JUNIOR GOLFERS

THE PARENTS GUIDE BOOK

GLEN BOWEN

JUNIOR GOLFERS
THE PARENTS GUIDE

DEDICATED TO MY GOLF STUDENTS
PAST, CURRENT, AND FUTURE

by
Glen Bowen

Certified Professional Golf Coach
United States Golf Teachers Federation

Champion Club Member
United States Golf Association

Additional Golf Books by Glen Bowen

Scoring Magic – Transform Your Short Game Today
Golf Decoded – Beginner's Guide
Mind Over Mulligan – Mastering Your Mindset
Golden Greens – Golfing Through Life's Back Nine
Optimization of the Golf Swing – Biomechanics
Ultimate Guide to Golf – The Journey Begins

Golfopedia Trilogy – Golf Deconstructed

Front Nine – Mastering Golf from Ace to Zip
Back Nine – Exploring the Science Behind Golf
Nineteenth Hole – Wrapping Up Your Final Round

Introduction

Welcome to "Junior Golf—The Parents Guide," a comprehensive resource designed to help you navigate the rewarding yet complex journey of supporting a young golfer. As parents, you play a pivotal role in your child's golfing experience, and this guide aims to equip you with the knowledge, strategies, and insights needed to make that role both effective and enjoyable.

Golf offers unique opportunities for young athletes that extend far beyond the fairways and greens. It's a sport that builds character, teaches life lessons, and creates lasting memories. However, the path of junior golf can sometimes feel overwhelming—from selecting the right equipment and finding appropriate coaching to managing tournament schedules and maintaining a healthy balance between competition and enjoyment.

Throughout this guide, you'll find practical advice on crucial aspects of junior golf development, including:

- Creating a supportive environment that nurtures your child's passion for the game
- Understanding the technical and mental aspects of golf
- Navigating tournaments and competitive play
- Building effective relationships with coaches
- Managing the balance between golf and other activities
- Supporting your child's physical and mental well-being
- Planning for potential collegiate golf opportunities

What sets this guide apart is its focus on the parent's perspective. While there are many resources available on golf technique and strategy, this book specifically addresses the challenges and opportunities you'll face as a parent of a junior golfer. Whether your child is just beginning their golf journey or competing at an advanced level, you'll find valuable insights to help you make informed decisions and provide the right kind of support.

Remember, every young golfer's journey is unique, and there's no one-size-fits-all approach to junior golf development. Use this guide as a framework to create an environment where your child can thrive, learn, and most importantly, enjoy the game. The chapters that follow will help you understand not just what to do, but why certain approaches work better than others in fostering long-term success and enjoyment in golf.

Contents

Guide for Parents

How Parents Can Support Their Junior Golfer

To effectively support a child in golf, parents should first understand the sport itself. Golf is not only about physical skill but also mental resilience, patience, and strategic thinking. Familiarizing themselves with the rules of golf, the structure of junior tournaments, and the basics of swing mechanics can help parents engage more meaningfully with their child's experience. This knowledge allows parents to provide informed feedback and encouragement.

Encouragement and Positive Reinforcement

One of the most crucial aspects of supporting a young player is providing consistent encouragement. Parents should celebrate their child's efforts rather than just outcomes. For instance, praising improvements in technique or effort during practice can foster a love for the game and reduce performance anxiety. Positive reinforcement helps build confidence, which is essential for young athletes as they navigate both successes and setbacks.

Creating a Supportive Environment

Parents can create an environment conducive to growth by ensuring that their child has access to proper coaching and training facilities. This might involve enrolling them in local golf clinics or hiring a qualified coach who specializes in junior golf development. Additionally, providing opportunities for practice—whether at home or on the course—can enhance skill development. Parents should also ensure that their child has access to appropriate equipment that fits their size and skill level.

Balancing Competition and Fun

While competition can be motivating, it's important for parents to maintain a balance between competitive play and enjoyment of the game. Encouraging participation in friendly matches or casual rounds with family can help keep the experience enjoyable. Parents should avoid placing undue pressure on their child to win; instead, they should emphasize personal improvement and enjoyment of the sport.

Promoting Physical Fitness

Golf requires physical fitness, including strength, flexibility, and endurance. Parents can support their young player by encouraging regular physical activity outside of golf practice. This could include activities like swimming, running, or even yoga to improve flexibility—all of which contribute positively to a golfer's performance on the course.

Teaching Life Skills Through Golf

Golf is an excellent platform for teaching valuable life skills such as discipline, respect for others (including opponents), sportsmanship, and time management. Parents should use golfing experiences as teachable moments where children learn about setting goals, handling disappointment, and working hard towards achieving objectives.

Involvement Without Overbearing Pressure

Parents should strive to be involved without being overbearing. Attending tournaments or practices shows support but should not translate into micromanaging their child's performance or decisions on the course. Allowing children some autonomy fosters independence and decision-making skills that are crucial both in sports and life.

Communication Is Key

Maintaining open lines of communication is vital for understanding how your child feels about their golfing journey. Regularly discussing their experiences—what they enjoy about playing golf or any challenges they face—can help parents provide tailored support that meets their child's emotional needs.

Setting Realistic Expectations

Finally, it's important for parents to set realistic expectations based on their child's age, skill level, and personal goals in golf. Understanding that every golfer develops at their own pace helps prevent frustration for both parent and child. Supporting them through ups and downs while keeping expectations grounded will lead to a healthier relationship with the sport.

Basics of the Game of Golf

Golf is a precision club-and-ball sport that involves hitting a ball into a series of holes on a course using as few strokes as possible. The game is played on a golf course, which typically consists of 18 holes, each with its own unique layout and challenges. Understanding the fundamental aspects of golf can greatly enhance the experience for both junior golfers and their parents.

The Objective of Golf

The primary objective in golf is to complete each hole in the least number of strokes. Players start from a designated tee area and aim to hit the ball into the hole located on the green at the end of each hole. The total score for a round of golf is calculated by adding up the number of strokes taken on each hole.

Basic Rules and Etiquette

1. Teeing Off: Each hole begins with players teeing off from a designated area. Players must hit their ball from within this area.

2. Strokes: A stroke is counted every time a player swings at the ball, regardless of whether they make contact or not.

3. Order of Play: The player with the lowest score on the previous hole tees off first on the next hole. On the putting green, the player farthest from the hole plays first.

4. Out of Bounds and Penalties: If a ball lands out of bounds or in a hazard (like water), there are specific rules that dictate how to proceed, often involving penalty strokes.

5. Respecting Other Players: Golf etiquette emphasizes respect for fellow players, including maintaining silence while others are taking their shots and repairing any damage made to greens or fairways.

Understanding Golf Terminology

Familiarity with common golf terms can help parents understand their child's experiences better:

- Par: The number of strokes an expert golfer is expected to take to complete a hole.

- Birdie: Completing a hole one stroke under par.

- Bogey: Completing a hole one stroke over par.

- Eagle: Completing a hole two strokes under par.

- Fairway: The well-maintained area between the tee box and green where grass is cut short for easier play.

Equipment Used in Golf

1. Clubs: Golfers use various types of clubs, including drivers (for long-distance shots), irons (for mid-range shots), wedges (for short approach shots), and putters (for rolling the ball into the hole).

2. Balls: Standard golf balls are designed for distance and control; they have dimples that affect aerodynamics.

3. Tees: Small devices used to elevate the ball above ground level when starting play on each hole.

4. Golf Bag: Used to carry clubs, balls, tees, and other accessories like gloves and rangefinders.

5. Apparel: Comfortable clothing suitable for outdoor play; many courses have dress codes that require collared shirts and appropriate footwear.

The Importance of Practice

For junior golfers, consistent practice is crucial for skill development. This includes:

- Practicing swings at driving ranges.
- Working on putting skills on practice greens.
- Playing rounds regularly to gain experience in different course conditions.

Parents can support their young players by encouraging practice routines, attending lessons with them, or simply playing together when possible.

By fostering an appreciation for golf's rules, etiquette, equipment, and practice habits, parents can create an enriching environment that encourages growth both as players and individuals.

Golf Course Strategies

Parents of junior golfers play a critical role in shaping their child's experience on the golf course.

Understanding the dynamics of the golf course, its environment, and how it impacts a junior golfer's development is essential for fostering a positive relationship with the game. Below are key areas parents should focus on when it comes to the golf course:

1. The Golf Course as a Learning Environment

The golf course is not just a place for competition; it is also an invaluable learning environment where juniors can develop life skills such as patience, discipline, decision-making, and resilience. Parents need to recognize that every round—whether good or bad—is an opportunity for growth.

- Encourage Exploration: Allow your child to explore different aspects of the game on the course without fear of failure. This includes experimenting with various shots, strategies, and approaches.

- Mistakes Are Part of Learning: Emphasize that mistakes made on the course are natural and provide valuable lessons. Avoid creating an atmosphere where errors are met with criticism or disappointment.

- Focus on Process Over Results: Teach your child to focus on process goals (e.g., maintaining proper form, staying calm under pressure) rather than just outcomes like scores or wins.

By treating the golf course as a classroom rather than solely a competitive arena, parents can help their children develop confidence and enjoy their time playing.

2. Understanding Course Management

Course management refers to how players navigate the challenges presented by each hole strategically. It is one of the most important skills for junior golfers to learn over time.

- Teach Patience and Strategy: Help your child understand that success on the golf course often comes from smart decisions rather than aggressive play. For example, choosing to lay up instead of attempting a risky shot over water can save strokes in the long run.

- Encourage Pre-Shot Planning: Support your child in developing routines for assessing each shot—considering factors like wind direction, hazards, pin placement, and club selection.

- Adaptability Is Key: Remind them that conditions on the golf course can change (e.g., weather shifts or varying green speeds), so adaptability is crucial.

Parents should avoid micromanaging their child's decisions during practice rounds or tournaments but instead encourage independent thinking and problem-solving.

3. Etiquette and Respect for Others

Golf is deeply rooted in traditions of etiquette and sportsmanship. Teaching junior golfers these values early ensure they grow into respectful players who understand the spirit of the game.

- Respect for Fellow Players: Teach your child to be mindful of others by avoiding distractions during another player's shot, repairing divots, raking bunkers after use, and marking their ball properly on greens.

- Pace of Play: Encourage efficient play without rushing—this includes being ready when it's their turn to hit and keeping up with the group ahead.

- Respect for Course Maintenance: Instill habits like fixing ball marks on greens and avoiding unnecessary damage to fairways or roughs.

Parents should model these behaviors themselves if they accompany their children during practice rounds or tournaments.

4. Emotional Management During Rounds

The emotional highs and lows experienced during a round can significantly impact performance. Parents must help their children learn how to manage emotions effectively while playing.

- Stay Calm Under Pressure: Teach your child techniques such as deep breathing or visualization to stay composed after poor shots or bad breaks.

- Avoid Overemphasis on Winning: Placing too much importance on results can lead to anxiety or frustration during rounds. Instead, celebrate effort and improvement regardless of score.

- Post-Round Reflection: After each round, encourage constructive reflection rather than dwelling on mistakes. Ask questions like "What did you do well today?" or "What could you improve next time?"

Parents should avoid expressing visible frustration during tournaments as this can add unnecessary pressure on young players.

5. Parental Behavior On-Course

How parents behave while watching their children play has a profound effect on performance and enjoyment.

- Be Supportive but Unobtrusive: Avoid coaching from outside the ropes during tournaments—it's against rules in most cases but also distracts players from focusing independently.

- Positive Body Language Matters: Children often look at their parents' reactions after shots; maintain encouraging expressions even if things aren't going well.

- Let Coaches Do Their Job: Trust professional coaches to handle technical feedback about swing mechanics or strategy rather than offering unsolicited advice mid-round.

By maintaining supportive yet hands-off behavior during rounds, parents allow juniors to take ownership of their game.

6. Familiarity With Tournament Rules

Junior golfers often participate in tournaments where understanding rules specific to competitive play is essential:

- Ensure your child knows basic rules such as penalty strokes for lost balls or unplayable lies.

- Familiarize yourself with tournament-specific guidelines (e.g., local rules) so you can support your child appropriately if questions arise.

Parents should also teach juniors how to self-report penalties honestly—a hallmark of integrity in golf—and ensure they know how scoring works in stroke-play formats commonly used in junior events.

7. Balancing Practice Rounds vs Competitive Play

Practice rounds are vital for preparing juniors for upcoming tournaments but should be approached differently than competitive rounds:

- Use practice rounds as opportunities for learning rather than focusing solely on scores.

  o Encourage notetaking about yardages, green slopes, hazard locations, etc., which will aid strategic planning later.

  o Experiment with different clubs off tees or around greens without fear of consequences since no official scorecard is involved.

Balancing structured practice sessions with fun recreational outings helps prevent burnout while keeping enthusiasm high.

For parents of junior golfers, understanding what happens both physically and emotionally on the golf course is critical for supporting their child's development effectively. By treating it as both a learning environment and an arena for personal growth—not just competition—parents can foster positive experiences that build confidence while teaching valuable life skills like patience, resilience, respect for others' efforts (and property), emotional regulation under stressors found within sport settings like tournament pressures alongside unpredictable environmental changes impacting gameplay itself.

Golf Equipment

When it comes to young players, selecting the right golf equipment is crucial for their development and enjoyment of the game. Parents play a significant role in this process, as they need to understand various aspects of golf equipment that can affect their child's performance and comfort on the course. Here's a detailed breakdown of what parents should know about golf equipment for young players.

1. Types of Golf Clubs

Junior golfers typically require clubs that are specifically designed for their size and strength. The main types of clubs include:

- Drivers: These are used for long-distance shots off the tee. Junior drivers are lighter and shorter than standard drivers, making them easier for young players to handle.

- Irons: These clubs are used for a variety of shots, from approach shots to chipping around the green. Junior irons come in sets that usually include 5-iron through pitching wedge, tailored to fit smaller hands and shorter swings.

- Wedges: Specialized clubs like sand wedges or lob wedges help with short-game situations around the greens.

- Putters: Essential for finishing holes, putters come in various styles. It's important to choose one that feels comfortable for the child.

Parents should ensure that clubs are fitted properly based on their child's height and strength. Many manufacturers offer fitting guides specifically for juniors.

2. Importance of Club Fitting

Young golfers should be fitted for golf clubs as soon as they begin showing interest in the game and are ready to start learning proper swing mechanics. Properly fitted clubs are essential for developing a solid foundation in their golf swing, as poorly fitted clubs can lead to compensatory movements that may hinder their progress and create bad habits that could last a lifetime.

The timing of fitting depends on the child's age, height, strength, and skill level. For very young children (toddlers or those under 6 years old), a basic set of lightweight clubs with minimal loft options may suffice. However, as children grow rapidly, it is important to reassess their equipment regularly—typically every 6-12 months—to ensure the clubs remain appropriate for their size and abilities. Once a junior golfer reaches around 60 inches (5 feet) tall or demonstrates advanced skills, they may transition to teen or adult-sized clubs with adjustments made for length and weight.

What Is the Process Involved in Fitting Junior Golfers?

1. **Measuring Height:** The first step in fitting junior golfers is measuring their height accurately. Junior golf clubs are often designed based on height rather than age because children of the same age can vary significantly in size.

2. **Assessing Swing Speed and Strength:** A club fitter will evaluate the child's swing speed and physical strength to determine the appropriate shaft flex and weight. Younger or beginner players typically require more flexible shafts and lighter clubheads to generate sufficient clubhead speed.

3. **Determining Proper Club Length:** The length of the club is critical for ensuring proper posture and swing mechanics. Clubs that are too long or too short can negatively affect balance, control, and accuracy.

4. **Choosing Shaft Flexibility:** Shaft flexibility must match the child's swing speed. Junior golfers generally benefit from more flexible shafts that allow them to achieve better distance without overexerting themselves.

5. **Selecting Grip Size:** Grip size is adjusted based on hand size to ensure comfort and control during swings. Grips that are too large or small can impede proper hand placement.

6. **Testing Lie Angle:** The lie angle—the angle between the shaft and the ground when the club rests flat—must be checked to ensure consistent ball contact during swings.

7. **Weight Considerations:** Junior clubs are designed with lighter heads compared to adult clubs so that younger players can handle them easily without straining their muscles.

8. **Skill Level Assessment:** Beginner juniors might start with ultralight sets featuring higher-lofted clubs (e.g., drivers with higher lofts, wedges) since these are easier to hit consistently. More advanced juniors might transition into sets with lower-lofted irons or hybrids as they develop better ball-striking skills.

9. **Growth Planning:** Since children grow quickly, many fitters recommend adjustable-length clubs or sets designed with growth in mind so that parents don't need to replace them frequently.

10. **Trial Swings:** Finally, junior golfers should test various options by taking practice swings under supervision from a professional fitter or coach who can observe their performance and make necessary adjustments.

Recommendations for Clubs and Brands for Junior Golfers

1. **US Kids Golf Clubs:**

- US Kids Golf is one of the most reputable brands specializing in junior golf equipment.

- Their clubs are proportionally sized based on height increments of 3 inches, making it easy to find an appropriate fit.

- They offer two main product lines:

    - *Ultralight Series*: Designed for beginner-to-intermediate players; these clubs are lightweight with flexible shafts.

    - *Tour Series*: Geared toward intermediate-to-advanced juniors; these feature slightly heavier heads and stiffer shafts for improved performance.

- Their grips come in nine progressive sizes tailored specifically for juniors' hands.

- US Kids Golf also provides fitting charts online (USKidsGolf.com) to help parents select suitable sets based on their child's measurements.

2. **Callaway XJ Junior Sets:**

- Callaway offers high-quality junior sets categorized by age groups (e.g., 5-8 years old, 9-12 years old).

- These sets include lightweight graphite shafts optimized for young players' swing speeds.

- Callaway XJ sets feature forgiving cavity-back irons and oversized drivers designed to boost confidence by making it easier to hit straight shots.

3. **Ping Prodi G Junior Clubs:**

- Ping's Prodi G line caters specifically to committed junior golfers who want premium-quality equipment similar to adult models but scaled down appropriately.

- These clubs use high-performance materials like titanium drivers and stainless steel irons while maintaining lighter weights suitable for juniors.

- Ping offers a unique "Get Golf Growing" program where parents can have their child's Prodi G set adjusted (e.g., lengthened) at no additional cost as they grow taller (Ping.com).

4. **TaylorMade Rory Junior Sets:**

- Inspired by professional golfer Rory McIlroy, TaylorMade created this line of junior golf sets aimed at encouraging young players.

- These sets include lightweight graphite-shafted woods, irons, wedges, putters, and bags designed specifically for kids aged 4-12 years old.

- TaylorMade focuses on creating forgiving designs that help beginners enjoy early success on the course (TaylorMadeGolf.com).

5. **Cobra King Junior Clubs:**

- Cobra offers junior-specific versions of its popular King series with features like lightweight construction and forgiving clubfaces.

- Their adjustable driver technology allows customization of loft settings as juniors improve their game (CobraGolf.com).

Additional Tips:

- Avoid using cut-down adult clubs because they tend to be too heavy even after shortening; this can lead to poor swing mechanics.

- For left-handed juniors, finding suitable equipment may require extra effort since fewer manufacturers produce left-handed options at affordable prices.

- Parents should involve children in selecting their equipment, so they feel invested in learning golf while enjoying personalized gear suited just for them.

3. Ball Selection

Choosing the right golf ball is also important for junior golfers. Generally, softer balls provide better feel and control, which can enhance learning:

- Distance Balls: Designed for maximum distance but may not provide as much spin or feel.

- Soft Compression Balls: These balls are easier to compress during impact, making them suitable for juniors who may not have developed full swing speed yet.

Parents should consider purchasing lower-cost balls until their child develops more skill and consistency.

4. Other Essential Gear

In addition to clubs and balls, there are other pieces of equipment that can enhance a young player's experience:

- Golf Bag: A lightweight bag with comfortable straps is essential for carrying clubs easily.

- Shoes: Proper footwear provides stability and traction; look for shoes designed specifically for golf.

- Gloves: A well-fitted glove can improve grip and prevent blisters during play.

Parents should encourage their children to take care of their equipment by cleaning clubs regularly and storing them properly after use.

5. Safety Considerations

Safety is paramount when it comes to junior golfers:

- Ensure that all equipment is age-appropriate and not overly heavy or cumbersome.

- Encourage proper warm-up routines before practice or play to prevent injuries.

Parents should also supervise practice sessions, especially when children are learning new skills or playing on busy courses.

6. Budgeting for Equipment

Golf can be an expensive sport; however, there are ways parents can manage costs effectively:

- Consider purchasing used or second-hand equipment from reputable sources.

- Look into junior golf programs that often provide access to rental equipment at reduced rates.

Investing in quality gear initially may not save money in the long run as children grow out of equipment quickly. You must be mindful of affordability versus playability.

With these key aspects of golf equipment, parents can make informed decisions that will support their young player's development while ensuring they have fun on the course.

Basic Golf Terminology

Parents of junior golfers should familiarize themselves with golf terms and terminology to better understand the game, support their child's development, and communicate effectively with coaches, instructors, and other players. Below is a detailed breakdown of key golf terms that parents should know, categorized into beginner, intermediate, and advanced levels. This knowledge will help parents guide their children as they progress in the sport.

Beginner Golf Terms

These are foundational terms that every parent should know to understand the basics of golf:

- Par: The number of strokes a skilled golfer is expected to take to complete a hole or course. For example, a par-4 hole means it should ideally take four strokes to finish.

- Birdie: Scoring one stroke under par on a hole (e.g., completing a par-4 hole in three strokes).

- Bogey: Scoring one stroke over par on a hole (e.g., completing a par-4 hole in five strokes).

- Mulligan: An informal term for taking another shot without penalty after an initial poor shot. Often used casually but not allowed in official play.

- Alignment: Refers to how the golfer positions their body and clubface relative to the target line before taking a shot. Proper alignment is crucial for accuracy.

- Backswing: The initial phase of the golf swing where the club is brought back from its starting position to generate power for the downswing.

- Chip: A short shot played near the green using minimal airtime and maximum roll toward the hole. Typically executed with wedges or short irons.

- Putt: A gentle stroke made on the green aimed at rolling the ball into the hole. It requires precision rather than power.

Intermediate Golf Terms

As junior golfers advance in skill level, parents may encounter more nuanced terminology:

- Fairway: The well-maintained area between the tee box and green where most golfers aim to land their shots.

- Rough: The longer grass surrounding fairways and greens that makes shots more challenging.

- Green: The smooth, closely mowed area around each hole where putting occurs.

- Dogleg: A hole that bends left or right instead of running straight from tee to green.

- Break: The curve or slope on a green that affects how a putt rolls toward the hole.

- Lie: Refers to how and where the ball rests on the ground (e.g., "good lie" means it's easy to hit; "bad lie" might mean it's buried in rough or sand).

- Hazard: Any obstacle such as water features (lakes/ponds) or bunkers (sand traps) designed to make holes more challenging.

Advanced Golf Terms

For parents whose children are competing at higher levels or playing competitively, understanding advanced terminology can be helpful:

- Draw/Fade: Controlled shots where the ball curves slightly left (draw) or right (fade) during flight for strategic positioning.

  o *Note*: For right-handed players, a draw curves left while a fade curves right.

- Hook/Slice: Unintentional severe curvatures during flight caused by improper swing mechanics:

  o *Hook*: Ball curves sharply left.

  o *Slice*: Ball curves sharply right.

- Sweet Spot: The optimal point on the clubface for striking the ball cleanly with maximum efficiency and minimal vibration.

Fun Slang Terms

Golf also has playful slang terms that add personality to conversations about gameplay:

1. Chilly Dip: A poorly executed chip shot where contact with the ground occurs before hitting the ball, resulting in insufficient distance.

2. Made an X: Humorously describes conceding a hole after struggling too much by picking up your ball without finishing it.

Why Learning These Terms Matters

Understanding these terms allows parents to:

1. Communicate effectively with coaches about their child's progress or areas needing improvement.

2. Support their child emotionally by discussing gameplay confidently without feeling out of place among other golfing families.

3. Encourage proper etiquette by teaching children how specific terms relate directly to rules or sportsmanship within golf culture.

By learning these terms early on, parents can foster an environment where junior golfers feel supported both technically and emotionally as they grow within this highly technical sport.

General Penalties in Golf

For junior golfers to succeed and enjoy the sport, it's crucial for their parents to understand the most important penalties in golf. This knowledge not only helps parents guide their children but also ensures that juniors develop a strong respect for the rules of the game. Below is an in-depth explanation of key penalties in golf that every parent should be aware of:

1. Understanding General Penalty Rules

In golf, penalties are applied when players breach specific rules outlined by the governing bodies such as the USGA (United States Golf Association) or R&A (The Royal and Ancient Golf Club). These penalties are designed to maintain fairness and uphold the integrity of the game. The most common types of penalties include:

- Stroke Penalties: Adding one or more strokes to a player's score.

- Loss of Hole: In match play, certain infractions result in losing a hole.

- Disqualification: Severe breaches can lead to disqualification from a round or tournament.

Parents should teach their junior golfers that understanding these consequences is essential for playing within the spirit of the game.

2. Key Penalties Every Parent Should Know

Here are some of the most important penalties junior golfers may encounter during play:

a) Out-of-Bounds or Lost Ball (Rule 18)

- If a ball is hit out-of-bounds or lost outside a penalty area, it results in a one-stroke penalty.

- The player must replay from where they last hit (stroke-and-distance rule).

- To avoid delays, juniors can use local rules allowing them to drop near where the ball was lost with an additional two-stroke penalty.

b) Penalty Areas (Rule 17)

- If a ball lands in a penalty area (formerly called water hazards), players have options:

  o Play it as it lies without penalty.

  o Take relief with a one-stroke penalty by dropping outside the penalty area at designated spots.

- Red stakes indicate lateral relief options, yellow stakes limit relief options to behind the hazard.

c) Unplayable Lies (Rule 19)

- A player can declare their ball unplayable anywhere on the course except in a penalty area.

- Options include:

  o Replay from where they last hit with a one-stroke penalty.

  o Drop within two club lengths no closer to the hole with one stroke added.

  o Drop back on a line between where their ball lies and the hole with one stroke added.

d) Hitting Another Player's Ball (Rule 6.3c & Rule 14.7a)

- Accidentally hitting another player's ball incurs no penalty if done unintentionally during stroke play but may require replacing balls correctly.

- In match play, hitting another player's ball on purpose could result in loss of hole.

e) Playing From Wrong Place (Rule 14.7a)

- If juniors play from an incorrect spot on purpose or due to ignorance, they incur two strokes in stroke play or lose the hole in match play.

f) Double Hit (Rule 10.1a)

- Previously penalized under older rules, double hits now carry no additional strokes beyond what was played—this change simplifies things for juniors.

g) Touching Sand in Bunkers Before Stroke (Rule 12.2b (1))

- Players cannot deliberately touch sand with their club before making contact with their ball unless removing loose impediments or taking practice swings outside bunkers.

- Breaching this rule results in a two-stroke penalty.

3. Common Mistakes Leading to Penalties

Parents should help junior golfers avoid these frequent mistakes:

a) Not Marking Balls Properly on Greens

Failing to mark balls correctly when lifting them on greens can lead to penalties under Rule 14.1c.

b) Slow Play Violations

Exceeding time limits for shots can result in warnings followed by stroke penalties under Rule 5.6a.

c) Incorrect Scorecards

Signing an incorrect scorecard leads to disqualification under Rule 3.3b (3). Juniors must double-check scores before submission.

4. How Parents Can Help Juniors Avoid Penalties

Parents play an essential role in ensuring junior golfers understand and follow these rules:

1. Encourage juniors to read and familiarize themselves with "The Rules of Golf" handbook provided by USGA/R&A.

2. Practice scenarios involving common penalties during training sessions, so juniors know how to handle them confidently during tournaments.

3. Emphasize honesty and self-reporting—core values that define golf as a sport built on integrity.

4. Teach juniors how to seek clarification from officials if unsure about any ruling during competitions instead of guessing or ignoring potential infractions.

5. Why Learning About Penalties Matters

Understanding golf's rules and associated penalties fosters discipline, sportsmanship, and confidence among junior players:

1. It reduces anxiety during competitive rounds since players know how to handle situations calmly without fear of accidental infractions ruining their scores.

2. It builds trust between players, coaches, officials, and parents by demonstrating respect for fair play principles.

3. It prepares juniors for higher levels of competition where strict adherence to rules becomes even more critical.

By equipping themselves with this knowledge early on, parents ensure that their children grow into well-rounded athletes who embody both skill and character on and off the course.

Coach and Parent Communications

When it comes to junior golfers, effective communication between parents and school golf coaches is critical for fostering a positive environment that supports the athlete's development. Parents should approach these interactions with respect, understanding, and a clear focus on their child's growth as both a golfer and an individual. Below are detailed guidelines and insights into what parents should learn and know about communicating with school golf coaches.

1. Understand the Role of the School Golf Coach

Parents must first recognize the responsibilities and priorities of school golf coaches. These professionals are not only tasked with improving players' technical skills but also managing team dynamics, fostering sportsmanship, and balancing academics with athletics.

Coaches often have limited time to address individual concerns due to their obligations to the entire team.

- Key Takeaway: Respect the coach's role as a leader of the team rather than solely focusing on your child's needs. Avoid micromanaging or overstepping boundaries.

- How to Apply This: Before approaching a coach, consider whether your concern is something that truly requires their attention or if it can be addressed through other means (e.g., discussing it directly with your child).

2. Approach Communication With Respect & Professionalism

When reaching out to a school golf coach, it is essential to maintain professionalism in tone and content. Coaches appreciate when parents communicate thoughtfully without being overly emotional or demanding.

- Do:
  - Schedule meetings in advance rather than approaching coaches spontaneously at tournaments or practices.
  - Use email or other formal communication channels for initial contact.
  - Be concise and specific about your concerns or questions.
- Don't:
  - Criticize coaching decisions regarding playing time, tournament lineups, or strategies during competitions.

- o Compare your child to other players on the team in discussions with the coach.

- Example Statement: "Coach [Last Name], I'd like to schedule some time to discuss how [Child's Name] can continue improving their short game during practice sessions."

3. Focus on Development Over Results

One of the most common mistakes parents make is emphasizing outcomes (e.g., scores, rankings) rather than long-term development. Coaches value parents who prioritize their child's growth as an athlete over immediate results.

- Why This Matters: Coaches are more likely to engage positively when they see that parents share their philosophy of building well-rounded athletes rather than pressuring them for quick wins.

- How Parents Can Support This Approach:

- o Ask questions like: "What areas should my child focus on improving?" instead of "Why didn't they play better in the last match?"

- o Encourage your child to take ownership of their progress by asking them what feedback they've received from the coach.

4. Respect Team Policies and Boundaries

Every school golf program has its own set of rules regarding parent involvement, player conduct, practice schedules, tournament participation, etc. Familiarizing yourself with these policies will help avoid unnecessary conflicts.

- Examples of Common Policies:

- o Restrictions on parental presence during practices or matches.

- o Guidelines for addressing grievances (e.g., waiting 24 hours after a competition before contacting the coach).

- How Parents Can Adapt:

  - o Review any handbooks or materials provided by the coach at the start of the season.

  - o Encourage your child to advocate for themselves by addressing minor issues directly with the coach before involving you.

5. Build Positive Relationships Through Supportive Actions

Parents who actively support both their child and the overall team create stronger relationships with coaches. Demonstrating appreciation for their efforts goes a long way toward fostering mutual respect.

- Ways to Show Support:

  - o Volunteer for team-related activities such as fundraising events or transportation coordination.

  - o Attend matches as a spectator without interfering in coaching decisions.

  - o Express gratitude through simple gestures like thanking them after tournaments or sending occasional notes of appreciation.

6. Avoid Overstepping: Let Your Child Take Ownership

As children grow older, especially in high school golf programs, it becomes increasingly important for them to take responsibility for communicating with their coaches about goals, challenges, or concerns.

- Why This Is Important: Coaches often prefer direct communication with players because it helps build accountability and independence—key traits for success both on and off the course.

- Parental Role:

  o Encourage your junior golfer to ask questions like: "What can I do differently during practice?" "How can I prepare better for upcoming tournaments?"

  o Step in only when absolutely necessary (e.g., if there is an unresolved issue affecting your child's well-being).

7. Address Concerns Constructively When Necessary

If you have legitimate concerns about coaching methods or decisions that may negatively impact your child (e.g., unfair treatment), approach these situations carefully:

1. Gather all relevant information before initiating contact—ensure you understand both sides of any issue.

2. Request a private meeting rather than discussing sensitive matters publicly at events.

3. Frame concerns constructively by focusing on solutions rather than assigning blame.

Example Statement: "Coach [Last Name], I've noticed that [Child's Name] seems unsure about their role during matches lately—how can we work together to help them feel more confident?"

8. Recognize That Coaches Are Human Too

Coaches juggle multiple responsibilities beyond just coaching golf— they may also teach classes, manage administrative tasks, and deal with personal challenges outside work. A little empathy goes a long way in building rapport.

Tip: If possible, acknowledge their hard work during busy times (e.g., tournament season) by expressing appreciation verbally or through small gestures like thank-you cards from players/parents collectively.

Conclusion

By understanding these principles—respecting boundaries, prioritizing development over results, maintaining professionalism in communication, supporting team policies, encouraging player independence, addressing concerns constructively when needed— parents can foster productive relationships with school golf coaches that benefit everyone involved: players thrive under reduced pressure; coaches feel supported; teams function cohesively; and parents gain peace of mind knowing they're contributing positively without overstepping boundaries.

Practice and Tournaments

Schedules

Parents of junior golfers play a crucial role in supporting their child's development in the sport. Understanding the typical schedule for after-school practice, special events, and tournaments is essential to ensure that the junior golfer has a balanced routine that promotes skill development, mental well-being, and academic success. Below is a detailed breakdown of what parents should know about these aspects.

1. After-School Practice Schedule

After-school practice is the foundation of a junior golfer's development. It typically involves structured sessions designed to improve technical skills, physical fitness, mental focus, and course management. Here's what parents should know:

a) Frequency and Duration

- Frequency: Most junior golfers practice 3-5 days per week after school. The number of sessions depends on their age, skill level, and competitive goals.

    o Beginners may start with 2-3 days per week.

    o Advanced or competitive players often practice 4-5 days per week.

- Duration: Each session usually lasts between 1.5 to 3 hours. This includes warm-up time, focused drills, short-game work (putting/chipping), full-swing practice at the driving range, and sometimes on-course play.

b) Components of Practice

A well-rounded after-school practice schedule includes:

1. Warm-Up (15-20 minutes): Stretching exercises or light cardio to prevent injuries.

2. Technical Drills (30-60 minutes): Focused work on specific areas such as grip, stance, swing mechanics, or ball flight control.

3. Short Game Practice (30-45 minutes): Emphasis on putting, chipping, bunker shots, and pitching since these account for a significant portion of scoring in golf.

4. Full Swing Practice (30-45 minutes): Hitting balls at the driving range with different clubs to refine accuracy and distance control.

5. On-Course Play (Optional – 9 holes): Some practices involve playing part of a round to simulate real tournament conditions.

c) Balancing Academics

Parents must ensure that golf practice does not interfere with academic responsibilities:

- Encourage time management by setting aside specific hours for homework before or after practice.

- Communicate with coaches if academic pressures require adjustments to the schedule.

d) Rest Days

Rest is critical for avoiding burnout or overuse injuries:

- At least one or two rest days per week are recommended where no golf-related activities take place.

2. Special Events: Clinics, Camps, and Workshops

Special events provide opportunities for junior golfers to learn from professionals, gain exposure to new techniques, and network with peers in the golfing community.

a) Golf Clinics

Golf clinics are short-term group training sessions led by experienced coaches or professional players:

- Typically held on weekends or during school holidays.

- Focus areas include advanced swing techniques, mental game strategies, or specific skills like bunker play.

- Clinics often last 2–4 hours per session.

b) Golf Camps

Golf camps are multi-day programs designed for intensive training:

- Held during summer vacations or holiday breaks.

- Camps can last from 3 days up to several weeks depending on the program.

- They combine technical instruction with physical conditioning sessions and competitive play simulations.

c) Mental Game Workshops

Workshops focusing on sports psychology help junior golfers develop resilience under pressure:

- Topics include managing nerves during tournaments, staying present between shots, and building confidence through visualization techniques.

d) College Exposure Events

For high school-aged juniors aspiring to play collegiate golf:

- Attend showcase events where college coaches scout talent.

- These events often include seminars about NCAA recruiting rules and eligibility requirements.

3. Tournament Participation

Tournaments are an integral part of a junior golfer's journey as they provide real-world experience in competitive settings.

a) Types of Tournaments

Junior golfers participate in various types of tournaments based on their skill level:

1. Local Club Tournaments: Ideal for beginners; these are low-pressure events hosted by local golf clubs.

2. Regional/State-Level Tournaments: Organized by state golf associations; these attract intermediate-level players looking for tougher competition.

3. National/International Tournaments: High-level competitions such as AJGA (American Junior Golf Association) events cater to elite juniors aiming for college scholarships or professional careers.

b) Frequency of Tournaments

Competitive juniors typically participate in:

- Local tournaments every few weeks during the season (spring/summer).

- Larger regional/national tournaments once every month or two depending on travel logistics.

c) Preparation Before Tournaments

Parents should help their child prepare both physically and mentally before tournaments:

1. Ensure proper rest leading up to the event.

2. Pack essentials like snacks/water bottles/golf gear ahead of time.

3. Encourage positive reinforcement rather than adding pressure about performance expectations.

d) Travel Considerations

For out-of-town tournaments:

1. Plan travel arrangements early (flights/hotels).

2. Budget for entry fees which can range from $50–$500 depending on the event level.

3. Be mindful of balancing schoolwork if travel requires missing classes – communicate with teachers beforehand.

4. Balancing Golf With Other Commitments

While golf can be demanding due to its time-intensive nature, it's important for parents to encourage balance in their child's life:

1. Promote participation in other sports or hobbies during off-seasons to avoid burnout while developing complementary skills like agility or teamwork.

2. Support social interactions outside golf so that children maintain friendships beyond their golfing circle.

3. Monitor signs of stress related to over-scheduling – adjust commitments, if necessary, without compromising long-term goals.

Summary:

1. After-school practices typically occur 3–5 times weekly with sessions lasting 1–3 hours focusing on technical drills, short-game work, full swings at the range, and occasional course play while balancing academics effectively.

2. Special events like clinics/camps/workshops offer unique learning opportunities outside regular practices while fostering personal growth through exposure to new experiences such as college showcases or mental game training workshops.

3. Tournament schedules vary based on skill level but generally involve local competitions every few weeks alongside periodic regional/national events requiring careful preparation/logistics planning by parents who must also prioritize maintaining balance across all aspects including academics/social life/rest periods throughout this journey toward golfing excellence!

Rules for Parents During Tournaments

Parents play a crucial role in the development of junior golfers, but their behavior and adherence to specific rules during tournaments can significantly impact their child's performance, emotional well-being, and overall experience. To ensure a positive environment for junior golfers, parents must understand and follow certain guidelines when attending tournaments. Below is a detailed explanation of what parents should learn and know about these rules.

1. Understand Tournament-Specific Rules for Spectators

Each golf tournament or organization (e.g., AJGA - American Junior Golf Association, PGA Junior League) has its own set of rules for spectators, including parents. These rules are designed to maintain fairness, uphold the integrity of the game, and create an atmosphere conducive to competition without undue pressure on players.

- Stay Outside Designated Areas: Most tournaments require parents to remain outside the ropes or designated spectator areas. This ensures that players can focus on their game without distractions or interference.

- No Coaching During Play: Parents are strictly prohibited from coaching or advising their child during a round. Offering advice on club selection, strategy, or any aspect of play is considered a breach of the rules and could result in penalties for the player.

- Silence During Shots: Parents must remain quiet while players are taking shots to avoid disrupting concentration.

- Respect Pace of Play: Parents should not walk ahead or lag behind groups as this may interfere with pace-of-play regulations.

Failure to adhere to these rules may result in warnings from tournament officials or even disqualification of the player.

2. Avoid Adding Pressure Through Behavior

Parents often unintentionally add pressure through their actions or words during tournaments. It's essential to adopt behaviors that support rather than hinder a junior golfer's performance:

- Refrain from Emotional Reactions: Avoid visible frustration, disappointment, or excessive celebration after your child's shots. Such reactions can increase anxiety and distract them from focusing on their next shot.

- Do Not Compare Your Child to Others: Comparing your child's performance with that of other competitors can undermine confidence and create unnecessary stress.

- Be Positive Regardless of Outcome: Focus on effort rather than results. For example, instead of saying "Why didn't you make that putt?" say "You gave it your best effort out there."

3. Respect Other Players and Their Families

Golf is a sport built on respect and etiquette—not just between players but also among spectators. As a parent:

- Avoid Distracting Other Players: Do not engage in loud conversations, use cell phones near play areas, or move around when others are preparing to take shots.

- Cheer Appropriately: Applaud good shots by all players in the group—not just your own child—to foster sportsmanship.

- Do Not Interfere with Officials: Allow tournament officials to handle rulings or disputes without parental involvement unless explicitly asked.

4. Be Prepared for Post-Round Conversations

The car ride home after a tournament is often one of the most emotionally charged moments for junior golfers. Parents should approach this time thoughtfully:

- Let Your Child Lead the Conversation: If they want to talk about their performance, listen attentively without criticism. If they prefer silence, respect that as well.

- Focus on Positives First: Highlight things they did well before discussing areas for improvement (if appropriate).
- Avoid Overanalyzing Every Shot: Excessive analysis can lead to frustration and diminish enjoyment of the game.

5. Familiarize Yourself with Tournament Etiquette

In addition to specific rules set by organizations, general golf etiquette applies equally to parents attending tournaments:

- Dress appropriately according to golf course standards (e.g., collared shirts).

- Arrive early but avoid crowding practice areas where players are warming up.

- Follow instructions from marshals or tournament staff promptly.

By modeling proper etiquette yourself, you set an example for your child about how respectful behavior is integral to golf.

6. Encourage Independence

One key goal in junior golf is fostering independence in young athletes so they can learn decision-making skills both on and off the course:

- Allow them to manage their own equipment (e.g., carrying their bag if required by tournament rules).

- Let them navigate challenges like bad weather conditions or tough lies without stepping in.

This independence builds resilience and confidence over time.

7. Know When It's Time to Step Back

While it's natural for parents to want their children to succeed, over-involvement can be counterproductive:

- Recognize signs that your presence might be adding stress rather than support (e.g., if your child seems tense when you're watching).

- Consider alternating attendance at tournaments with other family members if necessary.

Sometimes giving space allows juniors more freedom to perform without fear of judgment.

Summary

By adhering strictly to tournament-specific spectator rules, maintaining supportive behavior during rounds, respecting other competitors' experiences, fostering independence in young athletes, and being mindful about post-round interactions, parents can create an environment where junior golfers thrive both competitively and emotionally.

These principles help ensure that junior golfers develop not only as skilled athletes but also as individuals who enjoy the game long-term—free from unnecessary pressure or negativity stemming from parental involvement during tournaments.

Exciting Things Can Happen

Watching your child compete in a golf tournament can be an exhilarating experience, filled with moments of pride, suspense, and joy. Golf is a sport that combines skill, strategy, and mental toughness, and witnessing your child navigate these challenges can create unforgettable memories. Below are some of the most exciting things that can happen during such tournaments:

1. Witnessing a Personal Best or Milestone Achievement

One of the most thrilling moments for any parent is seeing their child achieve a personal best or reach a significant milestone in their golfing journey. This could include:

- **Shooting their lowest score ever:** Watching your child break their previous record for 18 holes is an incredible moment that reflects their hard work and dedication.

- **Completing a "clean card" round:** A clean card means playing all 18 holes without making a bogey—only pars and birdies. This level of consistency and focus is rare and highly rewarding to witness.

- **Making their first birdie or eagle in competition:** Seeing your child sink a long putt for birdie or hit an incredible shot to set up an eagle opportunity is electrifying.

These milestones not only showcase their progress but also boost their confidence as they continue to grow in the sport.

2. Watching Them Overcome Challenges

Golf is as much about mental resilience as it is about physical skill. Some of the most exciting moments come when your child faces adversity on the course but manages to persevere:

- **Recovering from a bad hole:** If they make a double bogey or worse on one hole but bounce back with strong play on subsequent holes, it demonstrates maturity and mental toughness.

- **Executing a difficult recovery shot:** For example, if they hit into trouble (e.g., deep rough, sand trap, or behind trees) but manage to pull off an impressive recovery shot to save par or minimize damage, it's both thrilling and inspiring.

- **Handling pressure situations:** Whether it's sinking a clutch putt on the final hole to secure a good score or staying composed during sudden-death playoffs, watching them thrive under pressure can be heart-pounding yet deeply rewarding.

3. Experiencing Moments of Pure Skill

Golf tournaments often highlight moments where players demonstrate exceptional skill. As a parent, witnessing these moments firsthand can be incredibly exciting:

- **Hitting long drives straight down the fairway:** Seeing your child unleash powerful yet accurate tee shots that rival those of more experienced players is always impressive.

- **Perfect approach shots:** Watching them land the ball close to the pin from long distances showcases precision and control.

- **Draining long putts:** Few things are more satisfying than seeing your child read the green perfectly and sink a challenging putt from 20+ feet away.

These moments remind you just how much effort they've put into honing their craft.

4. Observing Their Growth as Competitors

Competitive golf isn't just about scores—it's also about sportsmanship, strategy, and self-improvement. Some exciting aspects include:

- **Strategic decision-making:** Watching your child choose smart strategies—like laying up instead of going for risky shots—demonstrates maturity beyond just technical skills.

- **Displaying great sportsmanship:** Seeing them congratulate competitors after good shots or handle setbacks gracefully shows character development that extends beyond golf.

- **Learning from mistakes in real-time:** It's exciting to see them adapt mid-round by correcting errors (e.g., adjusting putting speed after misjudging greens early on).

These qualities reflect not only growth as golfers but also as individuals.

5. Sharing Emotional Highs Together

The emotional highs during competitive golf are unmatched:

- **Celebrating together after great rounds:** Whether it's hugs at the 18th green or high-fives after an amazing shot, sharing these joyous moments strengthens bonds between parent and child.

- **Cheering quietly from afar (with binoculars):** Even though parents must stay at least 50 paces away per junior golf rules, silently celebrating when they execute great shots adds excitement while respecting boundaries.

These shared experiences create lasting memories for both you and your young golfer.

6. Being Part of Their Journey Toward Bigger Goals

For many young golfers, competitive tournaments are steppingstones toward larger aspirations—whether it's qualifying for regional championships, earning scholarships, or even pursuing professional careers someday:

- If your child qualifies for higher-level events through strong performances in local tournaments, it's incredibly fulfilling to know you were there supporting them every step of the way.

Watching them achieve these goals provides immense pride as you see how far they've come since picking up their first club.

Conclusion

In summary, watching your child play competitive golf offers countless opportunities for excitement—from witnessing personal achievements like clean cards and birdies to observing their growth as resilient competitors who handle pressure with grace. The combination of skillful play, strategic thinking, emotional highs, and shared milestones makes every tournament memorable for parents who support their children while respecting boundaries on the course.

Things Can Go Wrong

Watching your child compete in a golf tournament can be an exciting and rewarding experience, but there are several things that can go wrong during the event. These issues often stem from unintentional actions by parents or spectators that disrupt the golfer's focus, violate tournament rules, or create unnecessary stress. Below is a detailed breakdown of potential problems and how they can negatively impact your child's performance.

1. Arriving Late to the Tournament

One of the most critical mistakes parents can make is not arriving at the course on time. Golfers need adequate time to warm up, practice putting, and mentally prepare for their round. If you arrive late:

- **Consequences:** The player may feel rushed and stressed, which can disrupt their pre-round routine and focus.

- **Penalties:** According to Rule 5.3a of the Rules of Golf, if a player is late to their tee time by less than five minutes, they incur a two-stroke penalty. If they are more than five minutes late, they are disqualified from the tournament.

To avoid this issue:

- Plan to arrive at least one hour before the tee time.

- Account for potential delays such as traffic or forgotten equipment.

2. Disrupting Your Child's Focus

Golf requires intense concentration, and even small distractions can lead to poor shots or mistakes on the course. Parents may unintentionally disrupt their child's focus by:

- Offering unsolicited advice or comments about their play.

- Making noise (e.g., talking loudly, using cell phones).

- Standing too close to the player during critical moments.

How This Affects Performance: Distractions can break a golfer's mental rhythm and cause them to lose focus on their game plan. Elite players rely on being in "the zone," where they maintain full concentration throughout their round.

Solution: Stay silent during play and maintain a respectful distance (at least 50 paces away) as required by junior golf rules.

3. Violating Spectator Rules

Many tournaments have strict rules for spectators regarding where they can stand or walk during play. Common violations include:

- Walking in the fairway instead of staying in designated areas like roughs or tree lines.

- Standing too close to greens or tee boxes.

- Interfering with other players' shots by being in their line of sight.

Consequences: Violating these rules could result in complaints from other players or officials, potentially leading to penalties for your child if it's deemed that you interfered with play.

Solution: Familiarize yourself with spectator guidelines before attending the tournament and follow them closely.

4. Over-Involvement During Play

Parents sometimes try to assist their child too much during tournaments by:

- Offering advice about club selection or strategy (which is prohibited under most amateur golf rules).

- Searching for lost balls without being asked by the player.

Consequences: Providing advice constitutes a breach of Rule 10.2a (1), which prohibits giving advice during play unless you are serving as an official caddie (which is rare in junior tournaments). This could lead to penalties against your child.

Solution: Only assist when explicitly asked by your child (e.g., helping spot errant shots). Otherwise, remain an observer.

5. Emotional Reactions That Add Pressure

Parents who show visible frustration or disappointment after bad shots may inadvertently increase pressure on their child. Examples include:

- Sighing audibly after missed putts.

- Criticizing decisions made during play.

Impact on Performance: This behavior can undermine your child's confidence and add unnecessary stress, making it harder for them to recover mentally after mistakes.

Solution: Maintain a calm demeanor regardless of how your child performs. Offer encouragement rather than criticism after rounds.

6. Mismanaging Errant Shots or Lost Balls

When a golfer hits into trouble areas (e.g., water hazards, deep rough), parents might instinctively start searching for balls without waiting for instructions from their child. This behavior can:

- Distract players who are trying to decide whether to hit a provisional ball.

- Waste valuable time since golfers only have three minutes under Rule 18.2a (1) to search for lost balls before incurring penalties.

Solution: Wait until your child asks for help before looking for lost balls and allow them space to make decisions about hitting provisional shots.

7. Failing to Respect Other Players' Space

Golf etiquette extends beyond just watching your own child; it also involves respecting other competitors in the group by:

- Avoiding conversations near other players while they're preparing shots.

- Not standing directly behind another player's line of sight when putting.

Consequences: Disrupting other players could lead to complaints filed with tournament officials and damage relationships within the golfing community.

Solution: Be mindful of all players on the course and follow proper golf etiquette at all times.

8. Equipment Mishaps Before/During Play

Forgetting essential items like clubs, gloves, tees, or even snacks/hydration supplies can derail preparation and performance during tournaments.

Impact: A missing club could force adjustments mid-round that affect scoring potential; lack of hydration could lead to fatigue later in play.

Solution: Double-check all equipment before leaving home and pack extras where possible (e.g., additional gloves).

9. Misinterpreting Rules About Provisional Balls/Scoring Assistance

Parents unfamiliar with golf rules might inadvertently give incorrect advice about playing provisional balls or scoring situations (e.g., penalty strokes). This misinformation could confuse young golfers during critical moments in competition.

Solution: Educate yourself about basic golf rules so you don't unintentionally mislead your child if questions arise mid-round

10. Visible Nervousness That Transfers Stress Onto Your Child

Children often pick up on their parents' emotions; if you appear overly nervous while watching them compete, it may increase anxiety levels for your young golfer as well.

Impact: Increased anxiety leads to rushed decisions or mechanical errors during swings due to tension buildup in muscles caused by stress hormones like cortisol.

Solution: Practice staying composed throughout rounds—your calm presence will help foster confidence in your child's abilities regardless of outcomes!

Parents and Limits of Assistance

Parents play a significant role in supporting their junior golfers, but there are specific limits and guidelines regarding the assistance they can provide during competitive golf tournaments. These rules are established by governing bodies such as Golf Canada, the USGA (United States Golf Association), and other tournament organizers to ensure fair play, maintain the integrity of competition, and foster independence among junior golfers. Below is a detailed explanation of these limits:

1. On-Course Coaching or Advice

Parents are generally prohibited from providing on-course coaching or advice during competitive rounds.

- According to Rule 10.2a (1) of the Rules of Golf, players must make decisions about their play independently without receiving advice from others during a round. "Advice" is defined as any counsel or suggestion that could influence a player's decision on club selection, shot type, or strategy.

- Parents may not caddy for their child unless explicitly allowed by the tournament rules.

- Violations of this rule can result in penalties for the player, ranging from stroke penalties to disqualification.

2. Physical Presence on the Course

Parents may be allowed to walk along with their child during tournaments but must adhere to strict spectator guidelines.

- Many junior golf tournaments permit parents to follow their children as spectators but require them to remain on designated paths or areas away from players.

- Parents are not allowed to interfere with gameplay by entering tee boxes, greens, or fairways unless explicitly permitted (e.g., in younger age divisions where parental assistance might be more lenient).

- Communication between parents and players is often restricted during play except for emergencies.

3. Equipment Assistance

Parents cannot assist with equipment decisions or adjustments once play has started.

- Players must carry their own bags or use caddies if permitted by tournament rules; parents cannot act as informal caddies unless specifically allowed.

- If a parent provides unauthorized equipment assistance (e.g., handing clubs mid-round), it could lead to penalties under Rule 4.3a (1), which governs equipment use and modifications.

4. Emotional Support and Encouragement

While emotional support is encouraged off-course, it must not disrupt gameplay or violate tournament etiquette rules.

- Parents should avoid excessive cheering, coaching gestures, or any behavior that could distract other players.

- Tournament officials may remove parents who fail to comply with these behavioral standards.

5. Financial Support and Logistical Arrangements

Parents can assist with financial and logistical aspects outside of actual gameplay but must respect deadlines and eligibility criteria set by organizers.

- For example, programs like the Canadian Junior Financial Assistance Program allow parents to apply for travel-related grants on behalf of their children but require adherence to application timelines.

- Once at the event venue, logistical support (e.g., transportation between hotel and course) is acceptable but should not extend into gameplay interference.

6. Compliance With Tournament-Specific Rules

Each tournament may have additional specific rules regarding parental involvement that must be followed strictly.

- Some events allow limited parental involvement for younger age groups (e.g., U15 championships) while enforcing stricter restrictions for older juniors.

- It is essential for parents to review tournament handbooks or websites before attending events.

7. Penalties for Violations

Violations of these limits can result in consequences such as:

1. Warnings issued by tournament officials.

2. Stroke penalties assessed against the player.

3. Disqualification from the event in severe cases.

To avoid issues, parents should familiarize themselves with both general golf rules (as outlined by governing bodies like the USGA) and specific tournament regulations provided by organizers like Golf Canada.

The Junior Golfer's Perspective

To understand how most children feel about parental participation during competitive golf tournaments, it is essential to consider the nuanced dynamics of parent-child relationships in the context of junior sports. The feelings of children toward their parents' involvement can vary widely depending on factors such as the level and type of support provided, the emotional climate created by parents, and the individual personality and preferences of the child. Below is a detailed breakdown of these dynamics:

1. Positive Feelings Toward Parental Support

Many children appreciate their parents' involvement when it is supportive, encouraging, and non-intrusive. Parents who act as quiet cheerleaders or steady supporters often foster a positive environment for their children. This type of involvement helps children feel emotionally secure and motivated without adding unnecessary pressure.

- **Emotional Support:** Children value unconditional love and encouragement from their parents, especially during high-pressure situations like tournaments. Statements such as "I'm proud of you" or "I loved watching you play" are particularly impactful in reinforcing confidence and reducing stress.

- **Presence Without Overbearing Behavior:** Simply being present at tournaments without micromanaging or criticizing allows children to feel supported without feeling judged.

- **Team Mentality:** When parents are seen as part of a "team" that includes coaches, mentors, and other supporters, children often view their involvement positively because it feels collaborative rather than controlling.

2. Negative Reactions to Overbearing or Critical Behavior

On the other hand, some children may develop negative feelings toward parental participation if it becomes overbearing or overly critical. This can lead to stress, resentment, or even burnout in young athletes.

- **Pressure from High Expectations:** When parents focus excessively on outcomes (e.g., winning or achieving a specific score) rather than effort, it can create anxiety for children. Comments like "You should win today" or "Why didn't you perform better?" can make them feel judged solely on their performance.

- **Criticism During or After Play:** Harsh feedback during car rides home or immediately after a round can be particularly damaging. Many junior golfers dread these moments if they anticipate criticism instead of constructive support.

- **Micromanagement:** Some children dislike when parents try to take control over aspects of their game (e.g., strategy decisions) that should be left to coaches or themselves.

3. Mixed Feelings Depending on Context

Children's feelings about parental participation are not always black-and-white; they may experience mixed emotions depending on specific circumstances:

- **Stress vs. Gratitude:** While some may feel stressed by having their parents watch every shot closely during a tournament, they might also appreciate knowing that someone cares deeply about their success.

- **Individual Preferences:** Some children thrive under close parental involvement while others prefer more independence during competitions.

4. Importance of Communication Between Parents and Children

One key factor influencing how children feel about parental participation is open communication between parent and child. According to experts in junior golf coaching:

- Many families fail to discuss how both parties feel about tournament dynamics, leading to misunderstandings.

- Encouraging honest conversations about expectations and boundaries can help align parental behavior with what the child finds helpful.

- A child might express that they prefer minimal interaction during rounds but enjoy discussing highlights afterward.

- Parents who listen empathetically and adjust their behavior accordingly are more likely to foster positive feelings in their child.

5. Long-Term Perspective: Building Confidence Beyond Golf

Ultimately, how a child feels about parental participation often depends on whether the parent emphasizes personal growth over athletic achievement:

- Children tend to respond well when parents prioritize character development (e.g., resilience, sportsmanship) over results.

- Reinforcing messages like "You're much more than just a golfer" helps reduce performance-related pressure while strengthening self-esteem.

In Summary: Most children appreciate parental participation in competitive golf tournaments when it is supportive yet non-intrusive. They value emotional encouragement, unconditional love, and presence without judgment. However, excessive pressure, criticism focused on outcomes rather than effort, or micromanagement can lead to negative feelings such as stress or resentment. Open communication between parents and children is crucial for ensuring that parental involvement aligns with what the child finds helpful.

School Golf Coach Participation

High school golf coaches are often involved in supporting their players during competitive tournaments, but there are specific rules and limitations they must adhere to. These rules are typically governed by the National Federation of State High School Associations (NFHS), state athletic associations, and the United States Golf Association (USGA) Rules of Golf. Below is a detailed explanation of the limits of assistance high school golf coaches can provide during competitive tournaments:

1. On-Course Coaching During Play

High school golf coaches are generally allowed to provide advice and guidance to their players during competitive rounds, but this is subject to strict limitations:

- **Designated Coaching Areas or Times**: Many state high school athletic associations allow coaches to give advice only in designated areas, such as near tee boxes or greens, or during specific times, such as between holes. For example, some states permit coaching only after a player has completed a hole and before they tee off on the next one.

- **Prohibition on Interference**: Coaches cannot interfere with play by entering hazards or greens unless explicitly permitted by tournament rules.

- **One-on-One Interaction**: In most cases, advice must be given directly to the player without disrupting other competitors.

The USGA Rule 10.2a (1) defines "advice" as any counsel or suggestion that could influence a player's decision about club selection, shot type, or strategy. While high school tournaments may modify these rules slightly for educational purposes, they still prohibit excessive interference.

2. Equipment and Rule Clarifications

Coaches can assist players with equipment-related issues and rule clarifications:

- **Equipment Issues**: Coaches may help players replace damaged clubs or balls if needed but cannot physically carry equipment for them during play unless local tournament rules allow it.

- **Rule Interpretations**: Coaches can explain applicable rules if a player is unsure about how to proceed in a situation (e.g., relief options under penalty areas). However, the final decision must be made by the player.

3. Prohibited Actions

There are clear restrictions on what coaches cannot do during tournaments:

- **Caddying**: Coaches are not allowed to act as caddies by carrying bags or assisting with physical tasks like raking bunkers.

- **Continuous Advice**: Providing constant advice throughout a round is prohibited; communication must be limited to approved times or locations.

- **Interfering with Opponents**: Coaches cannot engage with opponents' players in any way that might influence their performance.

4. Adherence to Local Rules

Each state's high school athletic association may have additional guidelines that further restrict coaching activities:

- Some states limit the number of coaches who can interact with players during tournaments.

- Others may require coaches to remain outside certain boundaries (e.g., cart paths) except when providing permitted advice.

It is essential for both coaches and players to familiarize themselves with these local regulations before participating in competitions.

5. Penalties for Violations

If a coach exceeds their allowable role during a tournament:

- The player may incur penalties under USGA Rule 10.2a for receiving unauthorized assistance.

- Repeated violations could lead to disqualification of the player or disciplinary actions against the coach under state association policies.

Conclusion

In summary, while high school golf coaches can provide valuable support through strategic advice and rule clarifications during competitive tournaments, their assistance is strictly regulated by NFHS guidelines, USGA Rules of Golf, and local state athletic association policies. They must operate within designated areas or times without interfering excessively in play or violating established boundaries.

Personal Golf Coach Limits

Personal golf coaches play a significant role in the development of junior golfers, but their involvement during competitive tournaments is strictly regulated by the rules of golf and tournament-specific policies. These rules are primarily governed by the United States Golf Association (USGA) and other governing bodies like the R&A, as well as specific tournament organizers such as the American Junior Golf Association (AJGA). Below is a detailed breakdown of what personal golf coaches can and cannot do during competitive golf tournaments:

1. On-Course Coaching Restrictions

The USGA's Rules of Golf explicitly limit coaching assistance during a round to ensure fairness and uphold the integrity of competition. Rule 10.2a (1) states that players must make decisions on their own without receiving advice from others, except for designated caddies. Here are the key points regarding on-course coaching:

- **Advice Prohibition:** Personal golf coaches are not allowed to provide advice to their students during a competitive round unless they are officially acting as the player's caddie. Advice includes recommendations on club selection, shot strategy, or any decision-making related to playing the course.

- **Definition of Advice:** According to Rule 10.2a (1), advice is defined as any counsel or suggestion that could influence a player's decision about how to play a hole or make a stroke.

- **Communication Limitations:** Coaches cannot communicate with players in any way that could be construed as giving advice during play. This includes verbal communication, hand signals, or written notes.

2. Role of Caddies

If a personal coach is serving as an official caddie for their student, they are permitted to provide advice under Rule 10.3b (3). However, this comes with its own set of limitations:

- A coach acting as a caddie must adhere to all rules governing caddie conduct.

- They cannot breach other rules (e.g., improving conditions affecting the stroke under Rule 8.1).

- Tournament organizers may impose additional restrictions on who can serve as a caddie (e.g., AJGA events often prohibit parents or personal coaches from acting as caddies).

3. Pre-Round and Post-Round Coaching

Coaches are allowed to assist their students before and after competitive rounds:

- **Pre-Round Preparation:** Coaches can help players develop strategies for tackling specific holes or hazards before the round begins. This includes reviewing yardage books, discussing weather conditions, and practicing specific shots.

- **Post-Round Analysis:** After completing a round, players can consult with their coaches to analyze performance and identify areas for improvement.

However, once the player tees off on their first hole until they complete their final hole of the round, direct coaching is prohibited unless within allowable roles (e.g., if serving as a caddie).

4. Practice Areas During Tournaments

Tournament organizers typically allow personal coaches access to practice areas (driving range, putting greens) before and after rounds:

- Coaches can work with players on swing mechanics, putting techniques, or mental preparation in these designated areas.

- Once players leave these areas for their starting tee time, all coaching must cease.

Some tournaments may restrict access to practice areas based on accreditation or event-specific policies.

5. Spectator Conduct Rules

If personal golf coaches attend tournaments solely as spectators (not serving as caddies), they must comply with spectator conduct guidelines established by tournament organizers:

- Spectators are generally required to maintain distance from competitors during play.

- Any attempt by spectators—including personal coaches—to offer advice or interfere with play may result in penalties for the player under Rule 10.2a (1).

For example:

- The AJGA enforces strict spectator policies prohibiting interaction between players and spectators during competitive rounds.

- Violations could lead to warnings or disqualification depending on severity.

6. Tournament-Specific Policies

Different organizations may impose additional restrictions beyond those outlined in the Rules of Golf:

- The AJGA prohibits parents and personal coaches from serving as caddies at certain events.

- Some junior tours allow limited interaction between players and personal coaches at designated checkpoints (e.g., after nine holes), but this varies widely by event.

It is essential for both players and their coaches to review tournament-specific guidelines carefully before participating.

Summary

In summary:

1. Personal golf coaches cannot provide advice during competitive rounds unless they are officially acting as the player's caddie.

2. Coaches can assist with pre-round preparation and post-round analysis but must cease all coaching once play begins.

3. Access to practice areas is generally permitted before rounds but subject to tournament-specific rules.

4. As spectators, personal golf coaches must avoid offering advice or interfering with play.

Violating these restrictions can result in penalties for both players and potentially disqualification from events.

Physical Fitness for Juniors

When it comes to junior golfers, physical fitness is a critical component that can significantly enhance their performance on the course. Parents play an essential role in supporting their child's physical development and ensuring they are fit for the demands of golf. Here's a detailed breakdown of what parents need to consider regarding physical fitness for young players.

1. Understanding the Physical Demands of Golf

Golf may seem less physically demanding than other sports, but it requires a unique combination of strength, flexibility, endurance, and coordination. The golf swing itself is a complex movement that engages multiple muscle groups and requires stability and balance. Therefore, understanding these demands is crucial for parents when guiding their children in physical fitness.

2. Importance of Strength Training

Strength training is vital for junior golfers as it helps build the necessary muscle strength to generate power during swings. However, it is important to approach strength training appropriately for their age and development stage:

- Bodyweight Exercises: For younger juniors, bodyweight exercises such as push-ups, squats, and lunges can be effective in building foundational strength without the risk of injury associated with heavier weights.

- Resistance Bands: These can be introduced as they provide resistance without heavy loads, allowing for safe strength training that can improve swing mechanics.

- Focus on Core Strength: A strong core is essential for maintaining balance and stability during swings. Exercises like planks and rotational movements can enhance core strength.

3. Flexibility and Mobility Training

Flexibility plays a crucial role in a golfer's ability to perform an effective swing. Parents should encourage their children to engage in stretching routines that focus on key muscle groups used in golf:

- Dynamic Stretching: Before practice or play, dynamic stretches (like arm circles or leg swings) can help warm up muscles.

- Static Stretching: Post-practice static stretching (holding stretches for 15-30 seconds) helps improve overall flexibility and aids recovery.

- Yoga or Pilates: These practices not only enhance flexibility but also promote body awareness and mental focus—both important aspects of golfing.

4. Endurance Training

While golf does not require the same level of cardiovascular endurance as sports like soccer or basketball, having good aerobic fitness can help junior golfers maintain energy levels throughout long rounds:

- Aerobic Activities: Encourage participation in activities such as swimming, cycling, or running at moderate intensity to build cardiovascular endurance.

- Interval Training: Short bursts of high-intensity activity followed by rest periods can also be beneficial in improving overall fitness levels.

5. Balance and Coordination Exercises

Balance is critical in executing a proper golf swing. Parents should incorporate exercises that enhance balance and coordination into their child's routine:

- Balance Drills: Simple exercises like standing on one leg or using balance boards can improve stability.

- Coordination Activities: Sports like tennis or basketball can help develop hand-eye coordination which translates well into golfing skills.

6. Nutrition and Hydration

Physical fitness goes hand-in-hand with proper nutrition and hydration:

- Balanced Diet: Ensure that young players consume a balanced diet rich in fruits, vegetables, lean proteins, whole grains, and healthy fats to support their energy needs.

- Hydration Practices: Encourage regular water intake before, during, and after playing to prevent dehydration—especially during hot weather conditions.

7. Rest and Recovery

Adequate rest is essential for young athletes to recover from training sessions:

- Sleep Requirements: Ensure that junior golfers get enough sleep each night (typically 8–10 hours) to support growth and recovery.

- Active Recovery Days: Incorporate lighter activity days where they engage in fun physical activities rather than intense training sessions.

By focusing on these aspects of physical fitness—strength training, flexibility work, endurance building, balance exercises, nutrition management, hydration practices, and adequate rest—parents can significantly contribute to their young player's development both on and off the course.

Nutrition for Young Golfers

Parents of junior golfers play a critical role in ensuring their children are properly fueled for both performance on the course and overall health. Nutrition is a cornerstone of athletic success and understanding how to implement a balanced diet tailored to the needs of young athletes can significantly impact their energy levels, recovery, focus, and long-term development. Below is a detailed breakdown of what parents should know about nutrition for junior golfers.

The Importance of Balanced Nutrition

Junior golfers require a well-rounded diet that includes all three macronutrients—proteins, carbohydrates, and fats—in appropriate proportions. This balance ensures sustained energy levels during practice or tournaments while supporting muscle recovery and overall growth.

Calories as Energy

Calories provide the energy needed for daily activities, including golf training and competition. The number of calories required depends on the child's age, weight, activity level, and growth stage. It's important to ensure that junior golfers consume enough calories to meet their energy demands without overloading on unhealthy foods.

Macronutrient Breakdown

o Proteins: Essential for muscle repair and recovery after physical activity. Protein intake should make up about 12-15% of total daily caloric intake. For junior golfers, this equates to approximately 0.64–0.82 grams per pound of body weight daily.

- Sources: Lean meats (chicken, turkey), fish (salmon), eggs, beans, lentils, tofu.

o Carbohydrates: The primary source of energy for young athletes. Carbohydrates should account for 55-60% of total caloric intake.

- Simple carbs (e.g., fruits) are ideal post-workout for quick energy replenishment.

- Complex carbs (e.g., whole grains, sweet potatoes) provide sustained energy throughout the day.

o Fats: Serve as a secondary energy source when carbohydrates are depleted. Healthy fats should comprise 25-30% of total caloric intake.

- Sources: Avocados, nuts/seeds (almonds, chia seeds), olive oil.

Hydration

Proper hydration is crucial for maintaining focus and physical performance during long rounds or practice sessions:

- Encourage consistent water consumption throughout the day—not just during play.

- During tournaments or hot weather conditions, supplement water with electrolyte drinks to replace lost minerals like sodium and potassium.

Pre-Round Nutrition

A pre-round meal sets the foundation for sustained energy during play:

- Timing: Eat 1.5–2 hours before tee time to allow digestion.

- Composition: Combine complex carbohydrates with protein while avoiding high-fat or sugary foods that may cause sluggishness or an energy crash.

  - Example Meal:
    - 2–3 scrambled eggs
    - Whole-grain toast
    - A cup of fruit (e.g., berries)
    - Water

Mid-Round Snacks

Golf rounds can last several hours; therefore, maintaining steady blood sugar levels is essential:

- Opt for snacks combining simple and complex carbohydrates with small amounts of protein.

- Avoid sugary snacks like candy bars that cause rapid spikes followed by crashes in energy levels.

  - Example Snacks:

    - Fresh fruit (e.g., apple slices)

    - Vegetables (e.g., carrot sticks)

    - Whole-grain crackers

    - Protein bars made from natural ingredients

    - Electrolyte powders mixed into water

Post-Round Recovery Nutrition

Recovery nutrition is often overlooked but vital after walking several miles over four to five hours:

1. Replenish glycogen stores with carbohydrates immediately after finishing the round.

2. Repair muscles by consuming protein within an hour post-play.

3. Rehydrate thoroughly with water or electrolyte drinks.

Example Post-Round Meal: Grilled chicken breast, Quinoa or brown rice, steamed vegetables, a piece of fruit

Nutritional Education

Parents should educate themselves and their children about making healthy food choices both at home and on the road during tournaments:

1. Teach kids how to read food labels to identify added sugars or unhealthy trans fats in processed foods.

2. Encourage them to choose whole foods over processed options whenever possible.

Special Considerations for Junior Golfers

Growth Spurts:

During periods of rapid growth (typically between ages 12–14), nutritional needs increase significantly due to heightened demands from both physical activity and development processes such as bone growth and muscle building.

Avoiding Early Specialization Pitfalls:

While golf-specific skills are important, parents should encourage participation in other sports during early developmental years (ages 5–12). This helps build "physical literacy"—a foundation of movement skills that supports long-term athleticism.

Individualized Needs:

Every child has unique dietary requirements based on factors such as metabolism rate, allergies/intolerances (e.g., lactose intolerance), or specific goals like weight management or muscle gain.

Avoiding Processed Foods:

Limit consumption of fast food or snacks high in trans fats as these can negatively impact performance by causing inflammation or sluggishness.

Mental Game Development

The mental game is a crucial component of golf, especially for young players who are still developing their skills and understanding of the sport. Parents play a significant role in fostering a positive mental approach to the game. Here's a detailed look at what parents need to know about mental game development for their junior golfers.

1. Importance of Mental Toughness

Mental toughness refers to a golfer's ability to maintain focus, confidence, and composure under pressure. For young players, developing this trait can significantly impact their performance on the course. Parents should encourage their children to embrace challenges and view setbacks as opportunities for growth rather than failures. This mindset helps build resilience, which is essential in competitive sports.

2. Goal Setting

Setting realistic and achievable goals is fundamental in developing a strong mental game. Parents should work with their youngsters to establish both short-term and long-term goals that are specific, measurable, attainable, relevant, and time-bound (SMART). For example, a short-term goal might be improving putting accuracy over the next month, while a long-term goal could involve qualifying for a specific tournament within the year. Regularly reviewing these goals can help maintain motivation and focus.

3. Visualization Techniques

Visualization is a powerful tool used by many successful athletes. Parents can teach their junior golfers how to visualize successful shots or rounds before they play. This technique involves imagining every detail of the shot—how it feels, looks, and sounds—thereby creating a mental blueprint that can enhance performance during actual play.

4. Developing Routine and Consistency

A consistent pre-shot routine can help junior golfers manage anxiety and improve focus during competition. Parents should encourage their children to develop personalized routines that they follow before each shot or hole. This routine might include deep breathing exercises, positive affirmations, or specific physical movements that signal readiness.

5. Managing Emotions

Golf is an emotional game; players often experience highs and lows throughout a round. Teaching young players how to recognize and manage their emotions is vital for maintaining performance levels.

Parents can help by discussing strategies such as deep breathing techniques or positive self-talk when faced with frustration or disappointment on the course.

6. Encouraging Positive Self-Talk

Positive self-talk involves replacing negative thoughts with constructive ones that promote confidence and focus. Parents should model this behavior by using encouraging language themselves and helping their children develop phrases they can use during play to boost morale (e.g., "I am capable," "I've practiced this shot").

7. The Role of Practice in Mental Development

Regular practice not only improves physical skills but also enhances mental resilience through repetition and familiarity with various situations on the course. Encourage your child to practice under different conditions—such as varying weather or playing against different skill levels—to prepare them mentally for competition.

8. Seeking Professional Guidance

Sometimes it may be beneficial for youngsters to work with sports psychologists or coaches who specialize in the mental aspects of golf. These professionals can provide tailored strategies that address individual needs and help young athletes develop coping mechanisms for stressors associated with competition.

9. Balancing Competition with Enjoyment

While competition is important for skill development, it's equally crucial that junior golfers enjoy the game itself. Parents should emphasize fun over results at younger ages to foster a lifelong love of golf rather than burnout from excessive pressure.

Parents of young golfers should prioritize mental game development by focusing on building mental toughness, setting goals, utilizing visualization techniques, establishing routines, managing emotions effectively, promoting positive self-talk, encouraging regular practice under varied conditions, considering professional guidance when necessary, and ensuring that enjoyment remains central to their child's golfing experience.

Finding a Golf Coach

When parents are seeking a quality golf coach for their youngster, there are several critical factors to consider. A well-chosen coach can significantly influence a young athlete's development, enjoyment of the game, and overall performance. Here's a detailed guide on what parents need to know:

1. Qualifications and Experience

The first step in finding a quality golf coach is to evaluate their qualifications and experience. Look for coaches who have:

- Professional Certifications: Coaches certified by recognized organizations such as the PGA (Professional Golfers' Association), LPGA (Ladies Professional Golf Association), or the USGTF [US Golf Teachers Federation] demonstrate a commitment to professional standards.

- Experience with Junior Golfers: It's essential that the coach has specific experience working with junior players. This includes understanding the physical and psychological needs of younger athletes.

- Playing Experience: A background in competitive play can provide valuable insights into training techniques and strategies.

2. Coaching Philosophy

Comprehending a coach's philosophy is crucial. Parents should inquire about:

- Teaching Style: Does the coach focus on fundamentals, or do they emphasize advanced techniques? A good balance is often necessary for juniors.

- Development Focus: The best coaches prioritize skill development over immediate results, fostering a love for the game while improving performance.

- Communication Skills: Effective communication is vital, especially when working with children. The coach should be able to explain concepts clearly and motivate young players positively.

3. Reputation and References

Researching a coach's reputation can provide insight into their effectiveness:

- Reviews and Testimonials: Look for feedback from other parents and players regarding their experiences with the coach.

- Success Stories: Inquire about past students' achievements, such as tournament wins or improvements in their game.

- References: Don't hesitate to ask for references from current or former students' parents.

4. Training Environment

The environment where coaching takes place can significantly impact learning:

- Facilities: Ensure that the coaching facility has adequate resources, such as practice greens, driving ranges, and technology like swing analysis tools.

- Location: Consider the convenience of travel for regular lessons; proximity can encourage consistent practice.

5. Trial Lessons

Before committing long-term, it's beneficial to schedule trial lessons:

- Assessment of Fit: Trial lessons allow both the parent and child to assess whether they feel comfortable with the coach's style and approach.

- Observation of Interaction: Parents should observe how the coach interacts with their child—this can reveal much about their teaching methods and rapport.

6. Cost Considerations

While cost shouldn't be the only factor in choosing a golf coach, it is an important consideration:

- Lesson Fees: Understand what typical rates are in your area; this will help gauge whether a particular coach's fees are reasonable.

- Value Over Price: Sometimes higher fees correlate with better facilities or more experienced coaches; weigh these factors carefully.

7. Commitment to Development

Finally, ensure that the chosen coach is committed not just to teaching golf but also to developing well-rounded individuals:

- Life Skills Instruction: Many top coaches incorporate lessons on sportsmanship, teamwork, resilience, and discipline into their training programs.

- Long-Term Vision: A good coach will work with both player and parent to set realistic goals that align with personal aspirations in golf.

By considering these factors carefully, parents can find a quality golf coach who will support their youngster's growth both on and off the course.

Encouraging Practice

For junior golfers, regular practice and play are essential for skill development, confidence building, and fostering a lifelong love for the game. Parents play a crucial role in encouraging their children to engage in both structured practice sessions and casual play. Understanding the balance between these two aspects can help parents create a supportive environment that nurtures their child's golfing journey.

Creating a Positive Environment

1. Supportive Atmosphere: It's vital for parents to cultivate an encouraging atmosphere where young golfers feel safe to express themselves and make mistakes. This means celebrating small victories, providing constructive feedback, and avoiding excessive criticism. A positive mindset can significantly enhance a child's motivation to practice.

2. Setting Realistic Goals: Help your child set achievable goals that focus on improvement rather than just winning or beating others. These goals can be related to specific skills (like improving putting accuracy) or performance metrics (such as lowering their score). Setting short-term goals can provide immediate motivation, while long-term goals keep them focused on continuous improvement.

Establishing a Routine

1. Regular Practice Schedule: Encourage your child to establish a consistent practice routine that fits into their weekly schedule. This could involve dedicated time at the driving range, putting greens, or playing rounds of golf. Consistency is key in developing muscle memory and honing skills.

2. Incorporating Variety: To keep practice engaging, introduce variety into their routine. This could include different drills focusing on various aspects of the game (driving, chipping, putting) or even playing different courses to experience diverse challenges.

Encouraging Social Interaction

1. Playing with Peers: Encourage your child to play with friends or join junior golf leagues where they can meet other young golfers. Social interactions not only make the game more enjoyable but also foster healthy competition and camaraderie.

2. Family Involvement: Participate in family golf outings where everyone plays together regardless of skill level. This not only strengthens family bonds but also allows younger golfers to see golf as a fun activity rather than just a competitive sport.

Promoting Mental Resilience

1. Teaching Patience and Persistence: Golf is a challenging sport that requires mental toughness and resilience. Teach your child that setbacks are part of the learning process and encourage them to remain patient during difficult times.

2. Mindfulness Techniques: Introduce mindfulness practices such as visualization techniques or breathing exercises that can help manage stress during play or practice sessions.

Utilizing Resources for Improvement

1. Professional Coaching: Consider enrolling your child in lessons with a qualified golf instructor who can provide tailored guidance based on their individual needs and skill level.

2. Educational Materials: Provide access to books, videos, or online resources about golf techniques, strategies, and mental approaches to enhance their understanding of the game.

3. Technology Integration: Utilize technology such as swing analysis apps or GPS devices that track performance metrics during practice rounds which can provide valuable feedback for improvement.

By combining these strategies—creating a positive environment, establishing routines, encouraging social interaction, promoting mental resilience, and utilizing resources—parents can effectively support their youngster's development both on and off the course.

Competitive Golf at an Early Age

Playing competitive golf at an early age can significantly influence a young golfer's development, skills, and overall enjoyment of the sport. Engaging in competition helps to cultivate not only technical abilities but also essential life skills such as discipline, resilience, and strategic thinking. This multifaceted approach to learning the game lays a strong foundation for future success both on and off the course.

Skill Development

One of the primary benefits of participating in competitive golf from a young age is the accelerated development of golfing skills. Young players are exposed to various playing conditions, course layouts, and competitive scenarios that challenge their abilities. This exposure allows them to refine their swing mechanics, putting techniques, and overall game strategy more rapidly than through casual play alone.

Competitive environments often require players to adapt quickly to different situations—such as varying weather conditions or pressure from opponents—which enhances their problem-solving skills. As they face these challenges repeatedly, they learn how to manage their emotions and maintain focus under pressure, which are critical components of successful performance in golf.

Mental Toughness and Resilience

Competing in golf teaches young players mental toughness—a crucial aspect of the game. Golf is inherently a sport that tests patience and perseverance; players must learn how to cope with setbacks such as poor shots or unfavorable outcomes. Early exposure to competition helps instill a growth mindset where failure is viewed as an opportunity for improvement rather than a reason for discouragement.

Moreover, dealing with the highs and lows of competition fosters resilience. Young golfers learn how to bounce back from disappointing rounds or missed opportunities, which builds character and determination. These traits are not only beneficial in sports but also translate into other areas of life, including academics and personal relationships.

Social Skills and Teamwork

Participating in competitive golf also enhances social skills. Young golfers interact with peers who share similar interests, fostering friendships that can last a lifetime. They learn valuable lessons about sportsmanship—how to win graciously and lose with dignity—which are essential qualities both on the course and beyond.

In team formats like junior leagues or school competitions, players develop teamwork skills that emphasize collaboration over individualism. They learn how to support teammates while also striving for personal excellence, creating a balanced perspective on competition that values both individual achievement and collective success.

Long-Term Commitment and Career Pathways

Engaging in competitive golf at an early age can set the stage for long-term commitment to the sport. Many successful professional golfers began competing as children; this early start often leads to greater opportunities for scholarships in collegiate golf programs or even professional tours later on. The discipline cultivated through regular practice and competition can lead young athletes toward pursuing careers related to golf—whether as professionals or in coaching roles.

Additionally, early involvement in competitive settings can help identify talent sooner. Coaches can spot potential early on and provide tailored training regimens that cater specifically to developing strengths while addressing weaknesses effectively.

In summary, playing competitive golf at an early age is vital for skill enhancement, mental fortitude, social interaction, and long-term engagement with the sport. The experiences gained through competition not only prepare young golfers for future challenges within the game but also equip them with life skills that will serve them well throughout their lives.

Playing for a School Team

1. Development of Skills and Techniques

Playing competitive golf on a school team provides students with structured opportunities to develop their golfing skills and techniques. Regular practice sessions, coaching from experienced instructors, and participation in matches help players refine their swings, putting, and overall game strategy. This environment fosters improvement through feedback and competition, allowing players to identify areas for growth and work systematically to enhance their performance.

2. Teamwork and Social Interaction

Being part of a school golf team encourages teamwork and camaraderie among players. Golf is often perceived as an individual sport; however, when played in a team context, it promotes collaboration and mutual support. Players learn to communicate effectively, strategize together during competitions, and celebrate each other's successes. This social interaction can lead to lasting friendships and a sense of belonging within the school community.

3. Mental Toughness and Resilience

Competitive golf challenges players not only physically but also mentally. The pressure of competition teaches students how to handle stress, maintain focus under challenging conditions, and develop resilience in the face of setbacks. Learning to cope with the highs and lows of competitive play can translate into valuable life skills that benefit students beyond the golf course.

4. Academic Benefits

Participation in sports like golf has been linked to improved academic performance among students. The discipline required for regular practice and competition can enhance time management skills, leading to better organization in academic pursuits. Additionally, being part of a school team often instills a sense of responsibility that encourages students to balance their athletic commitments with their studies effectively.

5. Health Benefits

Engaging in competitive golf promotes physical fitness among students. The sport involves walking long distances on the course, which contributes to cardiovascular health while also improving flexibility and coordination through various golfing movements. Furthermore, being active in sports can help combat sedentary lifestyles common among adolescents today.

6. Opportunities for Scholarships and Future Play

For many student-athletes, playing competitive golf at the high school level opens doors for college scholarships or opportunities to play at higher levels post-graduation. Many colleges actively recruit talented golfers who have demonstrated skill in high school competitions. This potential pathway can motivate students to excel both academically and athletically.

7. Lifelong Skills

Finally, participating on a school golf team instills lifelong skills such as discipline, goal setting, sportsmanship, and ethical behavior in competition. These attributes are essential not only in sports but also in personal development and professional environments later in life.

Playing competitive golf on a school team is significant for developing technical skills, fostering teamwork, enhancing mental resilience, promoting academic success, encouraging physical health, providing future opportunities for scholarships or advanced play, and instilling lifelong values.

Golf Competition Attendance

Attending tournaments is crucial for junior golfers, as it provides them with a supportive environment that can significantly enhance their performance and enjoyment of the sport. Parental attendance at competitions serves multiple purposes, including emotional support, logistical assistance, and fostering a positive competitive atmosphere.

Emotional Support

One of the primary roles parents play during tournaments is providing emotional support. Golf can be an intense sport, filled with pressure and competition. When parents are present, they can offer encouragement and reassurance to their child before, during, and after their rounds. This support helps to alleviate anxiety and boosts confidence. Studies have shown that athletes who feel supported by their families tend to perform better under pressure.

Logistical Assistance

Parents also play a vital role in logistics during tournaments. This includes transportation to and from events, ensuring that their child has all necessary equipment (clubs, balls, appropriate attire), and managing schedules. Being organized can reduce stress for both the parent and the golfer. Additionally, parents can help by preparing meals or snacks that provide energy without causing fatigue or digestive issues during competition.

Fostering a Positive Competitive Atmosphere

By attending tournaments, parents contribute to creating a positive atmosphere not just for their own child but for all competitors. Their presence can help cultivate sportsmanship values such as respect for opponents and appreciation for the game itself. Parents should model good behavior by cheering positively rather than criticizing or putting undue pressure on their child.

Encouraging Social Interaction

Tournaments are also opportunities for junior golfers to socialize with peers who share similar interests. Parents can facilitate these interactions by encouraging their children to engage with other players before or after rounds. Building friendships within the sport can enhance enjoyment and commitment to golf.

Comprehending Tournament Structure

Parents should familiarize themselves with how golf tournaments are structured. This includes understanding different formats (stroke play vs. match play), rules specific to junior competitions, and how scoring works. Knowledge of these elements allows parents to better support their child through informed discussions about strategy and performance expectations.

Managing Expectations

It is essential for parents to manage their expectations regarding outcomes in competitions. While it is natural to want one's child to succeed, emphasizing personal growth over winning can lead to a healthier mindset for young athletes. Encouraging effort, improvement in skills, and learning from experiences—whether wins or loses—can foster resilience.

Communication with Coaches

Maintaining open lines of communication with coaches is another critical aspect of supporting junior golfers at tournaments. Parents should engage with coaches regarding their child's progress and areas needing improvement while respecting the coach's authority in training decisions.

Post-Tournament Reflection

After each tournament, parents should take time to reflect on the experience with their child. Discussing what went well and what could be improved helps reinforce learning opportunities from each competition while celebrating achievements regardless of outcome.

Parental involvement in junior golf tournaments encompasses emotional support, logistical assistance, fostering a positive environment, encouraging social interaction among peers, comprehending tournament structures, managing expectations appropriately, maintaining communication with coaches, and engaging in post-tournament reflections.

Balancing Golf And Other Activities

Balancing sports, such as golf, with other activities is crucial for the holistic development of junior golfers. Parents play a significant role in this process, ensuring that their children not only excel in sports but also engage in academics, social activities, and personal interests. Here's a detailed breakdown of how to achieve this balance effectively.

1. Understanding the Importance of Balance

The first step in balancing sports with other activities is recognizing the importance of a well-rounded life. Engaging in various activities helps develop different skills and attributes:

- Physical Development: While golf enhances specific physical skills like coordination and strength, participating in other sports can improve overall fitness and agility.

- Mental Health: A diverse range of activities can reduce stress and prevent burnout associated with focusing solely on one sport.

- Social Skills: Interacting with peers through various activities fosters teamwork, communication skills, and friendships beyond the golf course.

2. Setting Priorities

Parents should help their youngsters set priorities based on their interests and commitments. This involves:

- Assessing Interests: Encourage children to explore different sports or hobbies to find what they enjoy most.

- Creating a Schedule: Develop a weekly schedule that allocates time for golf practice, schoolwork, family time, and leisure activities. This helps ensure that no single area dominates their time.

3. Encouraging Academic Commitment

Education is paramount for junior golfers. Parents should emphasize:

- Time Management Skills: Teach children how to manage their time effectively between studies and sports.

- Academic Support: Provide resources such as tutoring or study groups if needed to maintain academic performance while pursuing golf.

4. Promoting Physical Health

Maintaining physical health is essential for any athlete. Parents should encourage:

- Cross-Training Activities: Engage junior golfers in other physical activities (e.g., swimming, running) that complement their golf training.

- Nutrition Education: Educate them about proper nutrition to support both athletic performance and overall health.

5. Fostering Social Connections

Social interactions are vital for emotional well-being. Parents can facilitate this by:

- Encouraging Team Sports or Group Activities: Participation in team sports can enhance social skills and provide a break from individual competition.

- Family Time: Ensure regular family activities that do not revolve around sports to strengthen family bonds.

6. Monitoring Stress Levels

It's important for parents to be vigilant about their child's stress levels related to both academics and sports:

- Open Communication Channels: Maintain an open dialogue where children feel comfortable discussing pressures they may face.

- Recognizing Signs of Burnout: Be aware of signs indicating stress or burnout, such as decreased interest in golf or schoolwork.

7. Flexibility and Adaptability

Finally, maintaining flexibility within the schedule allows adjustments based on changing interests or commitments:

- Seasonal Adjustments: Understand that during peak golfing seasons, more time may need to be allocated to practice while still ensuring academic responsibilities are met.

- Reevaluating Goals Regularly: Encourage children to reassess their goals periodically—both in golf and other areas—to ensure they remain aligned with their evolving interests.

Balancing junior golf with other activities requires thoughtful planning and active involvement from parents. By fostering a supportive environment that values education, physical health, social connections, and flexibility, parents can help their young athletes thrive both on the course and beyond.

College-Bound
Junior Golf Programs

Parents of junior golfers aiming to help their children transition into collegiate golf programs need to understand the multifaceted process involved in preparing for college recruitment. This journey requires a combination of athletic, academic, and personal development strategies. Below is an in-depth guide to what parents should learn and know about college-bound programs for junior golfers who excel at competitive golf.

1. Understanding the College Golf Landscape

The first step for parents is understanding how collegiate golf operates in the United States. College golf is governed by organizations such as the NCAA (National Collegiate Athletic Association), NAIA (National Association of Intercollegiate Athletics), and NJCAA

(National Junior College Athletic Association). Each organization has its own set of rules, eligibility requirements, and levels of competition:

- NCAA Division I: The highest level of competition with rigorous academic and athletic standards. These programs often offer full or partial scholarships.

- NCAA Division II: Competitive programs that also provide scholarships but may have slightly less demanding schedules than Division I.

- NCAA Division III: Focuses more on academics; athletic scholarships are not offered, but other forms of financial aid may be available.

- NAIA and NJCAA: Offer opportunities for athletes who may not meet NCAA requirements or prefer smaller schools with strong athletic programs.

Parents should research which level aligns best with their child's skill level, academic goals, and personal preferences.

2. Academic Preparation Is Key

Colleges prioritize student-athletes who excel both on the course and in the classroom. Parents must ensure their child meets the following academic benchmarks:

- Core Course Requirements: The NCAA Eligibility Center mandates completion of specific core courses during high school (e.g., English, math, science).

- GPA Standards: A minimum GPA is required to qualify for collegiate athletics; this varies by division.

- Standardized Tests: SAT or ACT scores are critical components of eligibility. Parents should encourage early preparation through tutoring or practice exams.

- Time Management Skills: Balancing academics with competitive golf requires discipline. Parents can help by fostering good study habits early on.

Encouraging strong academic performance not only ensures eligibility but also opens doors to additional scholarship opportunities.

3. Building a Strong Golf Resume

A standout golf resume is essential for attracting college coaches' attention. Parents should assist their child in creating a comprehensive profile that highlights achievements both on and off the course:

- Tournament Results: Include scores from nationally ranked tournaments such as AJGA (American Junior Golf Association) events or state championships.

- Golf Handicap Index: A low handicap demonstrates consistency and skill.

- Swing Videos: High-quality videos showcasing different aspects of their game (e.g., drives, approach shots, putting) can be shared with coaches.

- Academic Achievements & Extracurriculars: Highlighting leadership roles or community service projects can differentiate your child from other recruits.

Parents should encourage participation in prestigious junior tournaments like AJGA events or USGA qualifiers to build credibility within the recruiting landscape.

4. Navigating the Recruiting Process

The recruiting process can be complex, so parents must familiarize themselves with key steps:

a) Start Early

Recruitment often begins as early as freshman or sophomore year in high school. Parents should encourage their child to start building relationships with college coaches early by attending camps, clinics, or showcases hosted by universities.

b) Communication With Coaches

Parents can guide their child on how to communicate professionally with coaches:

- Send personalized emails expressing interest in specific programs.

- Include tournament schedules so coaches can attend events where they're competing.

- Follow up after initial contact to maintain relationships.

c) Utilize Recruiting Platforms

Platforms like NCSA (Next College Student Athlete) or Junior Golf Scoreboard allow players to create profiles visible to college coaches. These platforms also provide tools for tracking rankings and finding suitable colleges based on skill level.

d) Official & Unofficial Visits

Parents should plan visits to campuses where their child is interested in playing:

- *Unofficial Visits*: Paid for by families; these visits allow players to explore campuses informally.

- *Official Visits*: Paid for by colleges; these visits typically include meetings with coaches and team members.

Understanding NCAA rules regarding contact periods (when coaches are allowed to communicate directly with players) is crucial during this stage.

5. Financial Planning

College golf can be expensive due to travel costs, equipment needs, coaching fees, and tournament entry fees during high school years. Parents must also consider tuition costs if scholarships do not cover all expenses:

a) Scholarships

Athletic scholarships vary widely depending on division level:

- Full scholarships are rare; most athletes receive partial awards covering tuition or housing.

- Academic scholarships can supplement athletic funding if your child excels academically.

b) Financial Aid

Filing the FAFSA (Free Application for Federal Student Aid) is essential for determining eligibility for federal grants or loans.

c) Budgeting During Recruitment

Traveling to tournaments where college scouts will be present requires careful budgeting. Parents should prioritize events that align with their child's goals while avoiding overspending on unnecessary competitions.

6. Mental Coaching & Emotional Support

The pressure associated with competitive golf and recruitment can take a toll on young athletes' mental health. Parents play a vital role in providing emotional support throughout this journey:

a) Focus on Effort Over Outcome

Encourage your child to focus on controllable factors like effort rather than stressing over results at every tournament.

b) Avoid Overbearing Behavior

While it's natural to want your child to succeed, being overly critical can harm their confidence. Instead, foster open communication about goals without imposing unrealistic expectations.

c) Hire Mental Coaches If Needed

Many junior golfers benefit from working with sports psychologists who specialize in performance anxiety management and goal-setting strategies tailored specifically for young athletes transitioning into collegiate sports.

7. Leveraging College-Bound Programs

Several organizations specialize in helping junior golfers navigate the path toward collegiate athletics:

- AJGA PBE Stars Program: The American Junior Golf Association offers Performance Based Entry stars that help players qualify for elite tournaments attended by college scouts.

- ForeCollegeGolf Programs: These services provide personalized guidance on everything from swing analysis videos to interview preparation tailored specifically toward aspiring collegiate golfers (ForeCollegeGolf).

- Junior Golf Scoreboard Rankings: This platform tracks player rankings nationwide based on tournament results—an important metric used by many recruiters (Junior Golf Scoreboard).

By leveraging these resources effectively alongside traditional recruitment methods like direct communication with coaches or campus visits mentioned earlier above ensures maximum exposure opportunities leading towards successful placements within desired institutions offering optimal growth potential academically and athletically alike.

Resources for Parents

Parents of junior golfers play a pivotal role in their child's development, not only as athletes but also as individuals. Beyond books about golf, there are numerous resources available that can help parents better support their children in the sport while fostering a healthy and balanced approach to competition, personal growth, and long-term success. Below is a detailed breakdown of key resources and areas parents should explore:

1. Mental Coaching Programs for Junior Golfers

One of the most critical aspects of golf is the mental game. Many junior golfers struggle with performance anxiety, fear of failure, or pressure from expectations. Parents can benefit from engaging with mental coaching programs designed specifically for young athletes. These programs often provide tools to help parents understand how their behavior impacts their child's mental state during competitions.

- Key Features:

  - Focus on reducing performance anxiety by teaching juniors to concentrate on process goals rather than outcomes.

  - Provide strategies for parents to lower expectations and foster confidence without adding pressure.

  - Help juniors develop resilience and emotional regulation skills.

- Examples of Resources:

  - Mental coaching platforms like Vision54 or Dr. Bhrett McCabe's "The MindSide" offer workshops and online courses tailored to junior golfers and their families.

  - The Positive Coaching Alliance (PositiveCoach.org) provides free downloadable guides and webinars for parents on fostering a positive sports environment.

2. Fitness Screening and Personalized Training Programs

Physical fitness plays an essential role in a junior golfer's development. Growth spurts during adolescence can lead to imbalances between muscle strength and bone growth, which may affect swing mechanics or cause injuries. Parents should consider resources that focus on physical conditioning tailored to young athletes.

- Key Features:

  - Physical screening assessments to identify flexibility, strength, or mobility issues.

- o Customized fitness plans that align with the child's developmental stage.

- o Emphasis on injury prevention through proper training techniques.

- Examples of Resources:

  - o Titleist Performance Institute (MyTPI.com): Offers certified junior golf fitness programs led by experts who specialize in biomechanics and youth athletic development.

  - o Local sports performance centers often provide youth-specific golf training programs focusing on core stability, flexibility, and endurance.

3. College Placement Guidance Services

For high school-aged juniors aspiring to play collegiate golf, navigating the college recruitment process can be overwhelming for both players and parents. Specialized services exist to guide families through this process effectively.

- Key Features:

  - o Assistance with creating player resumes (including tournament results) that appeal to college coaches.

  - o Advice on selecting tournaments that maximize exposure to recruiters.

  - o Insights into NCAA rules regarding recruiting timelines and scholarship opportunities.

- Examples of Resources:

- o Red Numbers Golf: Founded by former college coach John Brooks, this service mentors talented junior golfers through the college placement process while emphasizing long-term success beyond golf.

- o National Collegiate Scouting Association (NCSA Sports): Provides tools for connecting student-athletes with college coaches across various levels (Division I, II, III).

4. Online Communities and Forums for Junior Golf Parents

Connecting with other parents who are navigating similar experiences can be invaluable. Online communities allow parents to share advice, discuss challenges, and learn from others' successes.

- Key Features:

  - o Access to discussions about tournament preparation, equipment recommendations, or balancing academics with athletics.

  - o Opportunities to network with families whose children have successfully transitioned into collegiate or professional golf careers.

- Examples of Resources:

  - o Facebook groups such as "Junior Golf Parents" provide forums where members exchange tips about tournaments or coaching options.

  - o Websites like JuniorGolfHub.com include parent-focused articles alongside player development tools.

5. Equipment Fitting Services

Properly fitted equipment is crucial for young golfers as they grow rapidly during adolescence. Ill-fitted clubs can hinder swing mechanics or even lead to injuries over time. Parents should seek out professional club-fitting services that cater specifically to juniors.

- Key Features:

  - Clubs adjusted for weight, length, grip size, and shaft flex based on the child's current height/strength level.

  - Recommendations for equipment upgrades as the child grows physically stronger.

- Examples of Resources:

  - PGA Superstore locations often offer junior club fitting sessions conducted by certified professionals.

  - U.S.-based companies like U.S. Kids Golf specialize in lightweight clubs designed specifically for younger players.

6. Tournament Scheduling Platforms

Managing tournament schedules is another area where parents need support since playing too many events—or not enough—can impact a junior golfer's progress negatively. Tournament scheduling platforms help families find age-appropriate competitions while balancing practice time effectively.

- Key Features:

  - Searchable databases of local/regional/national tournaments categorized by skill level or age group.

      o   Tools for tracking tournament results over time (useful when applying for colleges).

- Examples of Resources:

      o   Junior Golf Scoreboard: Tracks rankings nationwide while listing upcoming events suitable for different age groups/skill levels.

      o   American Junior Golf Association (AJGA.org): Offers highly competitive events along with leadership programs aimed at holistic development beyond just golf skills.

7. Workshops/Clinics Focused on Parenting Young Athletes

Workshops designed specifically for sports parents teach valuable lessons about fostering healthy relationships between parent-coach-athlete dynamics while avoiding common pitfalls like over-involvement or excessive pressure.

- Key Features:

      o   Strategies for effective communication between parent-child-coach triads.

      o   Techniques for managing emotions during competitions (e.g., frustration after poor performances).

      o   Emphasis on building character traits such as perseverance rather than focusing solely on winning.

- Examples of Resources:

- o The Positive Coaching Alliance offers live workshops/webinars tailored toward parenting young athletes across all sports disciplines—not just golf (PositiveCoach.org).

- o Youth Sports Psychology seminars hosted by organizations like Winning Edge Academy focus heavily on parental roles in athlete mental health/development.

By leveraging these diverse resources—ranging from mental coaching programs to fitness training services—parents can create an environment where their junior golfer thrives both athletically and personally without succumbing unnecessarily high-pressure situations often associated with competitive sports environments today!

Additional Resources

American Junior Golf Association (AJGA)

Description: A premier organization dedicated to promoting competitive junior golf at national levels while offering resources about tournament schedules/recruitment pathways for aspiring collegiate/professional players.

PGA Junior League

Description: A program run by PGA professionals providing young golfers access to team-based competitions alongside structured coaching environments tailored toward skill-building within supportive communities nationwide.

US Kids Golf Foundation

A leading organization dedicated to promoting junior golf worldwide through tournaments, coaching programs tailored specifically toward younger athletes emphasizing fun-based skill-building approaches alongside parental education resources regarding best practices fostering healthy relationships between families & sport itself.

PGA.com (Professional Golfers' Association)

Offers expert insights into all aspects surrounding youth involvement within golfing communities globally—from beginner-friendly instructional tips aimed directly at kids themselves right through advanced-level advice geared towards helping guardians better navigate challenges arising throughout developmental stages encountered along journey toward mastery!

Positive Coaching Alliance:

A nonprofit organization dedicated to transforming youth sports culture by providing educational resources focused on positive reinforcement techniques for coaches/parents alike (PositiveCoach.org).

Titleist Performance Institute (TPI):

A leading authority in golf-specific fitness training offering certifications/programs aimed at improving athletic performance among players worldwide (MyTPI.com).

Red Numbers Golf:

A mentoring service founded by former NCAA coach John Brooks specializing in guiding talented junior golfers through developmental stages toward collegiate/professional success (RedNumbersGolf.com).

Drive, Chip, and Putt

The **Drive, Chip, and Putt (DCP)** program is a free nationwide junior golf development initiative aimed at growing the game of golf by focusing on three fundamental skills: driving, chipping, and putting. It was founded in 2013 as a collaborative effort between the Masters Tournament, the United States Golf Association (USGA), and The PGA of America. The program provides boys and girls aged 7-15 with an opportunity to compete in a fun and competitive environment while developing their golf skills.

Purpose and Goal

The primary goal of Drive, Chip, and Putt is to inspire young golfers by fostering their interest in the sport through creative competition. By focusing on the core aspects of golf—driving for distance, chipping for precision around the green, and putting for accuracy—

the program encourages skill development while promoting sportsmanship and camaraderie among participants.

Eligibility Criteria

1. Age Requirements:

o Open to boys and girls aged 7-15.

o Participants are grouped into four age categories: 7-9 years old, 10-11 years old, 12-13 years old, and 14-15 years old.

o Age is determined based on how old the participant will be on the date of the National Finals (April 6th, 2025).

2. Additional Rules:

o Participants must be at least 7 years old by April 6th of the competition year.

o A player turning 16 before April 6th is not eligible to participate.

o Proof of eligibility (e.g., birth certificate) is required for regional qualifiers.

3. Amateur Status:

o All competitors must adhere to USGA Rules of Amateur Status.

o Participation does not affect amateur status.

4. Equipment Compliance:

o Players' clubs and balls must conform to USGA equipment rules. However, certain restrictions regarding driver heads or groove specifications are not enforced for this competition.

Competition Structure

The Drive, Chip, and Putt competition consists of four stages:

1. **Local Qualifying:**

○ Held across all 50 U.S. states during May through July.

○ Up to three top point earners in each age/gender division advance to subregional qualifying.

2. **Subregional Qualifying:**

○ Conducted at approximately 60 sites during July and August.

○ Top two overall point earners in each division advance to regional qualifying.

3. **Regional Qualifying:**

○ Takes place at ten designated sites during September and October.

○ Winners from each division qualify for the National Finals.

4. **National Finals:**

○ Held annually at Augusta National Golf Club on the Sunday before The Masters Tournament.

○ This prestigious event is broadcast live on Golf Channel.

Each stage resets scores; there is no carryover from previous rounds.

Scoring System

Participants earn points based on their performance in three skill areas:

Driving:

- Players hit drives onto a fairway grid marked with boundary lines.

- Points are awarded based on both distance and accuracy within these boundaries.

Chipping:

- Players chip toward a target hole with concentric scoring circles around it.

- Points increase as shots land closer to the hole.

Putting:

- Players attempt putts from varying distances toward a target hole with scoring zones similar to chipping.

- Precision determines points earned.

The total score across all three disciplines determines rankings within each age/gender category.

Registration Process

1. Parents or guardians must register participants online via www.drivechipandputt.com.

2. Registration operates on a first-come-first-served basis until site capacity is reached.

3. Each participant may only register for one local qualifier; multiple registrations result in disqualification.

4. No entry fee is required for participation in any stage of Drive, Chip, and Putt competitions.

Key Dates for Upcoming Competitions

- Local Qualifying: May-July

- Subregional Qualifying: July-August

- Regional Qualifying: September-October

- National Finals: April 6th, 2025 (Sunday before The Masters)

In its upcoming edition (2025), eighty junior golfers representing various U.S states as well as Canada and India have qualified for the National Finals at Augusta National Golf Club—a testament to its growing international reach.

Unique Features

1. The National Finals take place at Augusta National Golf Club— one of golf's most iconic venues—making it an aspirational event for young golfers worldwide.

2. The competition fosters inclusivity by offering separate divisions for boys and girls across all age groups.

3. It emphasizes skill-building over financial barriers since participation is entirely free.

Understanding Golf's Unique Vocabulary

Golf, like many sports, has its own set of terms and phrases that can be confusing to those unfamiliar with the game. This specialized vocabulary serves not only to communicate effectively among players but also to create a sense of community and shared experience within the sport.

The Importance of Golf Terminology

Knowing the language of golf is essential for anyone looking to engage fully with the game, whether as a player, parent, coach, or spectator. Terms such as "worm burner," "hosel rocket," and "coast to coast flight" are just a few examples of how golfers describe their shots, strategies, and experiences on the course. Understanding these terms allows players to discuss their games more intelligently and helps parents and spectators better appreciate the nuances of play.

Building Connections Through Language

For many golfers, mastering this language is part of the social fabric of the sport. It fosters camaraderie among players who share similar experiences and challenges on the course. As one becomes more familiar with golf terminology, it opens up opportunities for deeper conversations about techniques, strategies, and even personal anecdotes related to golfing experiences.

In summary, understanding golf's unique vocabulary enhances both participation in and enjoyment of the game. It allows players to communicate effectively about their performance while also connecting with others who share their passion for golf.

The Secret Language of Golf Revealed

Above the Hole: This term refers to the position of a golf ball on a sloping green. When a golfer's ball is located in such a way that the next putt will be downhill, it is described as being "above the hole." This positioning can significantly affect the difficulty of the subsequent putt, as downhill putts generally require more precision and control.

Ace: An "ace" is a term used in golf to denote a hole-in-one. This remarkable achievement occurs when a golfer successfully hits the ball directly from the tee into the hole on their very first stroke. Scoring an ace is considered one of the most exciting moments in golf and is celebrated among players.

Address: The term "address" refers to the final stance or position that a golfer assumes just before executing their swing at the ball. Proper addressing involves aligning oneself correctly with both the ball and the target, ensuring that grip, posture, and stance are all conducive to making an effective shot.

Adjusted Gross Score: The adjusted gross score (AGS) is your total score after factoring in your handicap stroke allowance. This adjustment helps create a level playing field among golfers of varying skill levels by allowing less skilled players additional strokes based on their handicap, thus making competitions fairer.

Airmail: In golfing slang, "airmail" describes a shot that travels well beyond its intended target area. For instance, if a player's approach shot overshoots the green and lands in rough terrain behind it, this would be referred to as having "airmailed" the green. Such shots can lead to challenging recovery situations for golfers.

Albatross: An albatross, commonly referred to as a double eagle, represents an extraordinary achievement in the sport of golf. It occurs when a golfer completes a par-5 hole in just two strokes, which is an exceptionally rare feat even among seasoned players.

All Square: This term is used in match play scoring to indicate that the match is tied. When both competitors have won an equal number of holes, the status of the match is described as "all square."

Alternate Shot: This format involves two players who take turns hitting the same golf ball until it is holed out. Each player alternates their shots throughout the round.

Angle of Attack: The angle of attack refers to the trajectory at which a golf club approaches the ball at impact. A steep angle of attack indicates a sharply downward motion, while a shallow angle suggests a flatter approach.

Approach Shot: A shot that is typically short to medium in distance, aimed at the putting green or the pin. This type of shot is commonly known as an "approach shot."

Army Golf: This term refers to a golfer whose shots frequently alternate between veering left and right, mimicking the movement pattern of soldiers marching (left, right, left).

Attend the Flag: A customary practice in golf where one player holds the flagstick in place and then removes it while another player prepares to putt.

Attest: In the context of tournament play, this term signifies the act of both a player and a fellow competitor signing a scorecard to verify that the recorded scores are correct.

Away: The phrase "You're away" indicates that a player's ball is the farthest from the hole, which typically means it is their turn to take a shot.

Back Nine: This term describes the final nine holes on an eighteen-hole golf course.

Backspin: This refers to the reverse spin that is applied to a golf ball, which helps prevent it from rolling forward after it lands on the green. This effect is often referred to as "bite," as it allows the ball to stop quickly upon landing.

Back in the Stance: This term describes a golfer's positioning of the ball closer to their back foot than their front foot during the address phase. This technique is commonly employed when hitting wedges, as it can help achieve a higher trajectory and better control over short shots.

Bag Drop: A bag drop is a designated area, typically located near the entrance of a clubhouse, where golfers can unload their clubs upon arrival. This allows players to leave their equipment while they find parking or prepare for their round.

Ball Mark: A ball mark is the indentation left on the green when a golf ball lands. It indicates where the ball has impacted the surface and can affect subsequent putts if not repaired properly.

Ball Speed: Ball speed is influenced by several factors, including the velocity of the club head at impact and how close to the sweet spot of the club face the ball was struck. Higher ball speeds generally result in greater distances traveled by the golf ball through the air.

Ball Marker: A ball marker is a small object used to indicate the position of a golf ball that has been lifted from the green. Common items such as coins are frequently utilized as ball markers.

Banana Ball: The term "banana ball" is a lighthearted slang expression referring to the trajectory of a golf ball that has been sliced. A slice occurs when the ball curves from left to right during its flight, resembling the shape of a banana.

Barkie: A "barkie" is a term used in golf to describe a situation where a golfer strikes a tree with their shot but still manages to achieve par on that hole.

Beach [Bunker]: In golfing terminology, "beach" or "bunker" refers to sand traps located on the course. These hazards are filled with sand, and players must be cautious not to ground their club before hitting the ball out of them.

Bell: A bell is utilized on golf fairways to signal when it is safe for groups behind to hit their approach shots, particularly after the group ahead has cleared the green. The ringing of the bell serves as an alert for players waiting to tee off or take their next shot.

Below the Hole: This term describes the location of a golf ball on a sloped green. When a golfer's ball is positioned such that the next putt will be uphill, it is referred to as being "below the hole." This positioning can influence putting strategy, as uphill putts generally require more force than downhill ones.

Best Ball: In this format, partners or teams play using only the best score recorded for each hole. Each golfer plays their own ball throughout the round, but at the end of each hole, only the lowest score among team members is counted as the team's score for that hole. This format encourages teamwork while allowing individual performance to shine.

Birdie: A birdie is achieved when a golfer scores one stroke under par on a specific hole. This indicates that the golfer performed exceptionally well relative to the expected standard for that hole.

Bite: The term "bite" refers to backspin applied to a golf ball, which causes it to stop quickly upon landing with minimal or no roll afterward. This technique is often used by golfers to control their shots and improve accuracy on approach shots and greens.

Bladed Shot: A bladed shot occurs when the club head makes improper contact with the ball, striking it at its equator with the leading edge of the club. This type of shot is also referred to as a "skulled" shot. As a result of this mishit, bladed shots tend to travel much lower and often farther than the golfer intended.

Bogey: In golf terminology, a bogey refers to a score that is one stroke over par for a specific hole. This indicates that the player took more strokes than the established par to complete that hole.

Blind Draw: A blind draw is a method used in competitions where players' names are randomly selected without prior knowledge or bias for pairing them together in matches.

Break: The term break describes the curvature or slope of a putting green, which influences how a putt will roll toward its target. This effect is caused by variations in elevation and the contours present on the green.

Breakfast Ball: The breakfast ball is an informal rule in golf that permits players to take an additional shot at their first tee-off without incurring any penalty. This practice is commonly accepted as a way to help golfers start their round on a positive note.

Bunker: A bunker is classified as a hazard on the golf course, typically characterized by a depression filled with sand. In some cases, bunkers may also be grassy depressions, serving as obstacles for players during their game.

Buried Lie: This term refers to a situation in golf where a ball is "plugged" or "embedded" either in a bunker or on any other part of the course. If the ball is embedded in the fairway or rough, the Rules of Golf permit the player to lift the ball and take relief without incurring a penalty. However, if the buried lie occurs within a penalty area or bunker, players are required to play the ball as it lies. Alternatively, they may declare it an "unplayable lie," which results in a one-stroke penalty.

Cabbage: This slang term describes extremely thick and deep rough that can be very difficult for golfers to escape from when their ball lands in it.

Caddy: A caddy is an individual who carries and manages a golfer's clubs during play. In addition to carrying equipment, caddies often assist players with selecting clubs and developing strategies for their shots.

Car/Cart Fee: This refers to the charge incurred for utilizing a golf cart during a round of golf.

Car [or Golf Car]: This term denotes the vehicle employed for transportation on a golf course. The two predominant types of golf cars are electric powered, which operate quietly, and gas-powered, which produce engine noise upon acceleration.

Cart Path Only: This is a temporary restriction that some golf clubs impose on golfers using carts. During inclement weather or wet conditions that could potentially harm the course, club management may require that cart drivers remain exclusively on designated paved cart paths throughout their round.

Casting: This term describes an early release of the wrist hinge during the downswing, resulting in a throwing motion that leads to a notable decrease in both power and control.

Casual Water: This term refers to any temporary accumulation of water on the golf course that is not classified as a water hazard and is visible either before or after a golfer takes their stance. If a player's ball lands in casual water, they are permitted to lift it and relocate it to the nearest point of relief without incurring any penalty.

Chili-Dip: A chili-dip occurs when a golfer mishits a chip shot by making contact with the ground before hitting the ball, resulting in a shot that travels only a short distance.

Chicken Stick: This term refers to a golfer's dependable club that they feel confident using to achieve solid contact and consistent performance on the course.

CHIN: An acronym for the Golf Handicap Information Network, CHIN is an online tool provided by the USGA that allows golfers to manage their handicaps by posting scores and maintaining an official handicap record.

Chip Shot: A chip shot is characterized as a short stroke with a low trajectory aimed at landing the ball on the green, allowing it to roll toward the hole upon landing.

Chippie: The term chippie describes the successful act of chipping the ball into the hole from around the green area.

Chunk [Fat] Shots: A chunk, often referred to as a "fat" shot, occurs when the golf club strikes the ground before making contact with the ball. This results in a significant divot being taken out of the turf, and typically leads to a shot that falls short of the intended target. The primary reason for this type of shot is usually improper swing mechanics or poor timing, where the player makes contact with the ground instead of hitting the ball cleanly.

Thin [Skinny] Shots: Conversely, a "thin" or "skinny" shot happens when the lower part of the clubface makes contact with the ball. This type of strike can propel the ball further than intended because it often results in less loft being applied to the shot. Players may experience thin shots due to an overly steep swing path or lifting their head too early during their swing.

Clubhead Speed: Clubhead speed refers to how quickly the club head is moving at the moment it strikes the golf ball, measured in miles per hour (mph). This metric is crucial because higher clubhead speeds generally lead to increased "ball speed," which significantly influences how far a golfer can hit the ball. Faster clubhead speeds allow for more energy transfer from the club to the ball, resulting in longer distances.

Club Face: The club face is located on the front part of the club head and features a flat surface that typically includes horizontal grooves designed to enhance grip on the ball upon impact. The angle and orientation of the club face at impact are vital for determining both direction and distance of each shot.

Coast-to-Coast Flight: This term refers to the act of hitting a golf ball from one bunker to another bunker across the green, demonstrating a notable lack of distance control.

Compression: When a fast-moving golf club strikes a golf ball, the ball undergoes a momentary compression, where it is partially "squished" by the clubface. This compression is not visible to the naked eye; however, high-speed photography has shown that the ball does indeed experience this phenomenon upon impact, which contributes to its subsequent flight at a high velocity.

Condor: A condor is defined as achieving a score of 4 under par on a single hole. This occurrence is exceedingly rare and can be likened to making a hole-in-one on a par-5 hole.

Course Rating: The Course Rating provides a numerical assessment of how challenging a golf course would be for a "scratch" golfer. It often differs from the total par of the course due to variations in overall length and difficulty level. For instance, if a golf course has a par of 72 but boasts a course rating of 73.2, it indicates that the course presents significant challenges, suggesting that an expert player would likely score above par.

Clubhead: The clubhead is the part of the golf club that is specifically designed for making contact with the golf ball. It is typically located at the end of the club and plays a crucial role in determining the direction, distance, and trajectory of the shot.

Course: In golf, the term "course" refers to the entire area designated for play. This encompasses all the holes, fairways, greens, roughs, hazards, and any other features that are part of a golf facility where players can engage in the game.

Cut: The term "cut" in golf has three distinct meanings:

1. **Shot Type:** The first meaning pertains to a specific type of shot characterized by a controlled movement from left to right. Unlike a slice—which is an unintended and often erratic shot—the cut is executed intentionally by golfers who aim for this particular trajectory.

2. **Grass Height Levels:** The second usage relates to the varying heights of grass on a golf course after a ball has exited the fairway. The "first cut" refers to the area of grass immediately adjacent to the fairway, which is slightly longer than that found on the fairway itself. In contrast, the "primary cut" denotes areas further away from the fairway where grass is significantly longer.

3. **Tournament Format:** The third definition involves tournament play, specifically referring to a 4-day event where players must achieve certain performance standards during initial rounds. Only those who meet or exceed these standards qualify to advance into subsequent rounds of competition.

Daily Fee Course: A high-quality public golf course that is owned privately but accessible to the general public without any restrictions.

Dance Floor: This term refers to the putting green, where golfers aim to position their balls as close to the hole as possible, representing the area where all the action in putting culminates.

Defeated Flight: This term describes a secondary group of players who have lost their matches in the first round of a tournament.

Dew Sweeper: A colloquial term for golfers who play early in the morning, often while there is still dew on the grass.

Divots: These are chunks of turf that are removed from the ground when a golfer strikes the ball. It is important for players to replace these divots and step on them, or if a seed mix is available (check your golf cart or tee box), to fill in the hole completely.

Dogleg: This term describes the configuration of golf holes that curve in one direction or another, resembling the bend in a dog's hind legs. When a hole curves to the right, it is designated as a "dogleg right," while a hole that curves to the left is known as a "dogleg left."

Dormie: In match play golf (as opposed to stroke play), a player or team is termed "dormie" when they are ahead by as many holes as there are holes left to play. For instance, if a player leads by three holes with three holes remaining, they are considered dormie.

Double Bogey: A double bogey indicates that a golfer has taken two strokes more than the par for that hole. For example, on a par-4 hole, scoring 6 would be classified as a double bogey. To minimize the risk of achieving this score, golfers should focus on avoiding penalty strokes.

Double Cross: This situation arises when a golfer plans to execute one type of shot (such as fading) but inadvertently hits another type (like hooking), resulting in unpredictable and often unfavorable outcomes.

Double Eagle: This term refers to a score that is three strokes under par on a specific hole. For instance, achieving a hole-in-one on a Par 4 hole qualifies as a double eagle, as does scoring 2 on a Par 5 hole. This remarkable achievement is also known as an Albatross and is recognized as the second rarest shot in golf, with estimated odds of occurring at approximately 6 million to 1.

Down: In the context of match play (a format where players compete to win individual holes), a player who has lost more holes than they have won is described as being "down" in the match. For example, if a player has won two holes but lost four, they are considered "two down." This terminology helps convey the current standing of players relative to each other during the match.

Downswing: The downswing represents the latter part of a full golf swing. After completing the backswing (the initial phase where the golfer raises the club), there is a transition where the golfer begins the downswing. This involves returning the club head towards the ball at high speed in preparation for impact, which is crucial for generating power and accuracy in the shot.

Draw: In golf, this term can refer to two concepts. Firstly, it describes a method of pairing players or teams for competitions (see "pairings"). Secondly, it denotes a specific ball flight pattern where the ball curves to the left (for right-handed golfers) during its trajectory.

Drop: A drop refers to the procedure of returning the ball to play after a player has taken relief from either a penalty area or an unplayable lie. To execute a drop, the player must hold the ball at knee height and allow it to fall freely to the ground. Once the ball has been dropped in this manner, it is deemed back in play.

Driving Range: Also known as the 'practice range,' this is a designated area on a golf course, or a separate facility specifically designed for golfers to practice their swings. Players can purchase bags or buckets of golf balls to hit, eliminating the need to retrieve them after each shot.

Duck Hook: A duck hook is an exaggerated version of a hook shot that results in the ball making a sharp turn to the left. This type of shot often elicits laughter from other players due to its extreme nature and unpredictability.

Duff: The term "duff" describes a poorly executed shot in golf, indicating that it was struck very badly (e.g., "He really duffed that shot."). The term has also led to the slang usage of "duffer," which refers to an unskilled golfer.

Duffer: A casual golfer who has not yet perfected their swing technique, resulting in higher scores during play. This type of golfer often enjoys the social aspect of the game, which may include consuming beer while on the course.

Eagle: An eagle is a golf score that occurs when a player completes a hole two strokes under par. Although still considered a rare accomplishment, eagles are more frequently achieved than holes-in-one (aces) or three-under-par scores (albatrosses). Typically, eagles are made on par-5 holes where a golfer can reach the green in two strokes and successfully make the putt.

Elevated Green: An elevated green refers to a putting surface that is situated higher than both the fairway and the surrounding terrain. Players must hit an uphill shot to reach this green, adding an extra challenge to their approach.

Embedded Ball: An embedded ball occurs when a golf ball lands in such a way that part of it sinks below ground level, becoming lodged in its own pitch mark. This situation can affect how players proceed with their next shot, as specific rules apply to embedded balls during play.

Even Par: This term refers to a scenario in golf where a player completes a hole using the same number of strokes as the hole's par rating, or when their total score for 18 holes equals the overall par rating for the entire course. For instance, if a golfer scores a 4 on a hole designated as a Par 4, this is classified as "even par." Similarly, achieving a total score of 72 on a course with a par of 72 is also considered even par.

Executive Course: An executive course is significantly shorter than a standard full-length 18-hole golf course. These courses typically feature shorter Par 3 and Par 4 holes, resulting in fewer total yards. This design allows players to complete their rounds in less time compared to traditional courses.

Fade: The fade, sometimes called a "cut," is characterized by a golf shot that exhibits a slight curve in its trajectory from left to right (for right-handed golfers). This type of shot can be strategically used to navigate around obstacles or position the ball favorably on the green.

Fairway: The fairway consists of closely mown grass that extends from the tee box to the green. It represents the ideal area for golfers to land their shots, as it provides optimal conditions for subsequent strokes.

Fairway Woods: Fairway woods are specialized golf clubs designed for longer shots. They are typically employed as the initial shot on shorter par 4 holes or for second shots on par 5 holes. While they resemble drivers, fairway woods have smaller club heads, are slightly shorter in length, and possess more loft, making them suitable for various situations on the course.

Fat: This term refers to a mishit golf shot where the club strikes the ground before making contact with the ball. This results in grass or dirt being interposed between the ball and the clubface, which significantly reduces the distance the ball travels. Such shots are often colloquially known as "chunked" shots.

Flag Stick: The flag stick is a movable pole that features a flag at its top, placed in the hole on the green. Its primary purpose is to indicate the location of the hole to players on the course.

Flights: In golf, flights refer to groups of players who are bracketed together based on their qualifying scores or seeding. This organization helps manage competitions by ensuring that players of similar skill levels compete against one another.

Flop Shot: A flop shot is characterized as a high and soft shot that lands gently on the green. Typically executed using a lob wedge or sand wedge, this type of shot requires considerable skill and precision, often associated with accomplished golfers such as Phil Mickelson.

Flyer: When grass gets between the club face and the ball, particularly on shots taken from the rough, it can reduce friction, which in turn diminishes the backspin applied to the ball. As a result, these shots may come out with increased velocity, travel farther than anticipated, and roll significantly after landing. This phenomenon is referred to as a "flyer."

Fly The Green: The phrase "fly the green" describes a golf shot that overshoots its intended target area entirely. For instance, if a golfer's approach shot lands well past the putting surface and into the rough behind it, this is termed as having "flown the green."

Foot Wedge: This humorous slang refers to an instance where a golfer uses their foot to nudge their ball from a challenging lie to make their next shot more manageable. It is widely recognized among golfers that this practice is against the rules of golf.

Fore: This term is shouted as a warning to alert others on the course that a player's ball is heading in their direction and could potentially hit someone.

Forward Tees: Most golf courses feature multiple tee boxes from which players can drive the ball. The "forward tees" are positioned closest to the fairway, resulting in the shortest overall length of the hole when players opt to tee off from these boxes.

Four Jack: This term is slang for a situation in which a golfer takes four putts to complete a hole, indicating a struggle with putting.

Foursome: This term refers to a group of four golfers playing together during a round of golf. In contrast, a "threesome" denotes three golfers, a "twosome" indicates two golfers, and "single" refers to one golfer playing alone.

Free Drop: Under specific circumstances outlined in the Rules of Golf, players are allowed to relocate their ball without incurring a penalty stroke. The Rules also specify how this "free drop" should be executed.

Fried Egg: A "fried egg" in golf refers to a challenging situation where the ball is partially buried in a bunker, resembling the appearance of a fried egg. This scenario demands a high level of skill and finesse from the golfer, as executing a successful shot can be difficult due to the need to generate spin while dealing with the sand's resistance.

Fringe: The fringe is an area of grass that surrounds the green, typically cut slightly higher than the grass on the green itself. While landing on the fringe does not count as being on the green in regulation play, golfers often treat it similarly when putting. A common technique used on or around the fringe is the chip shot, where players utilize a wedge to gently bump and roll the ball towards the hole.

Frog Hair: Commonly referred to as "fringe," frog hair describes the strip of grass that encircles the putting surface. The height of frog hair is longer than that of the grass on the green but shorter than that found in the rough areas adjacent to it. This distinction helps golfers understand how to approach shots taken from this area.

Front Nine: The term "Front Nine" denotes the first nine holes of an 18-hole golf course. Specifically, holes numbered 1 through 9 are categorized as the Front Nine, while holes numbered 10 through 18 are known as the Back Nine. Understanding this division is essential for golfers when discussing their rounds or strategizing their play.

Gimme: A "gimme" in golf refers to a short putt that players agree can be counted as made without the need for the player to actually hit the ball into the hole. This informal agreement is typically based on the proximity of the ball to the hole, and it serves as a courtesy among players, allowing them to save time and effort during a round.

Golf: The term "golf" has its origins in Scotland, where it first appeared in a statute from 1457. The word is believed to derive from an older concept meaning "to strike" or "to cuff." Golf is played on a specially designed course and involves hitting a ball into a series of holes using clubs, with the objective being to complete each hole in as few strokes as possible.

Golf Bag: A golf bag is an essential accessory for golfers, typically made from materials such as leather, vinyl, or canvas. It is designed to carry golf clubs, balls, and various accessories needed during play. Golf bags come in different styles, including stand bags and cart bags, catering to different preferences and playing conditions.

Golf Glove: A golf glove is worn primarily on the left hand (for right-handed players) to enhance grip on the club. Wearing a glove helps prevent slippage during swings, especially in adverse weather conditions like rain or when hands are sweaty. This added grip contributes significantly to better control and accuracy while playing.

Golf Shoes: Golf shoes are specifically engineered footwear designed for playing golf. They feature specialized soles that provide traction necessary for maintaining balance during swings while also ensuring comfort throughout the game. The design of golf shoes often includes spikes or other gripping mechanisms that help prevent slipping on grass surfaces.

Grand Slam: The PGA Tour's four major championships consist of the Masters, the U.S. Open, the PGA Championship, and The Open Championship. A player who wins all four of these prestigious events within a single calendar year is recognized as having achieved the "Grand Slam."

Green: This area of the golf hole is specifically designed for putting and represents the most meticulously maintained section of the golf course.

Greens Fee: This term refers to the fixed amount that a golf club charges players for access to its course, allowing them to play either 9 or 18 holes.

Green In Regulation (GIR): Commonly abbreviated as GIR, this statistic indicates when a golfer reaches the green in the expected number of strokes relative to par. For example, a player achieves GIR by reaching the green in one stroke on a Par 3 hole, in two strokes on a Par 4 hole, or in three strokes on a Par 5 hole.

Greenskeeper: This individual is responsible for maintaining and caring for the golf course. Their duties include mowing grass, managing irrigation systems, applying fertilizers and pesticides, and ensuring overall course quality.

Grip: The grip refers to the portion of the golf club that a golfer holds. Common materials used for grips include leather and rubber, which provide varying levels of comfort and traction. Additionally, the term "grip" encompasses how a golfer positions their hands on the club, which is crucial for effective swing mechanics.

Grooves: Grooves are the horizontal indentations found on the face of a golf club. Their primary function is to enhance friction when the club strikes the ball, enabling the ball to achieve backspin during its flight. This backspin can significantly affect the ball's trajectory and landing behavior on the green.

Grounding Your Club: Grounding your club involves allowing the club head to make contact with the ground behind the ball before initiating your swing. According to golf rules, players are permitted to ground their clubs in areas such as fairways or roughs; however, this practice is not allowed when the ball is situated in a sand trap.

Ground Under Repair: This term refers to any section of a golf course that has been designated by course management as unplayable. Such areas are typically marked with white paint, indicating that players must remove their balls from these zones and drop them at the nearest point of relief without incurring any penalties.

Gross Score: A player's gross score refers to the total number of strokes taken during their round of golf, without any modifications for handicap calculations.

Hacker: This term is used pejoratively to describe a golfer who possesses limited skills and typically has a high handicap, indicating their level of play. Hackers may also be called "duffers."

Handicap: A golf handicap is a numerical measure that reflects a player's average performance relative to par, allowing golfers of varying abilities to compete on an equitable basis.

Hazard: In golf terminology, a "hazard" encompasses any area such as bunkers or water hazards that poses a challenge to players.

Head-to-Head: This term refers to the competition between two players or teams, evaluated on a hole-by-hole basis. It is commonly known as match play, where each hole is treated as a separate contest, and the player or team that wins the most holes wins the match.

Heel: In golf terminology, the heel is the part of the club face that is located closest to where the golf shaft connects to the club head. This area is crucial for understanding how different strikes can affect ball trajectory and distance. The opposite end of the club face is known as the "toe."

Hit: The term "hit" describes when a player makes contact with the golf ball. It encompasses various types of strokes, particularly distinguishing between a controlled stroke, such as putting, and a more aggressive hit that may lack precision and distance control. The latter often occurs when a player rushes their putt.

Hole: A hole in golf consists of several components: it includes a teeing ground from which players start their play, a putting green where the hole is located, and all areas in between. Additionally, "hole" can refer specifically to the physical hole on the green into which players aim to sink their ball.

Hole-In-One: A hole-in-one occurs when a golfer successfully hits their tee shot directly into the hole with just one stroke. This remarkable achievement is also referred to as an ace and is celebrated for its rarity and skill involved.

Honor: The term "honor" refers to the player who is designated to tee off first on a hole in golf. This is typically determined by the order of play established at the start of the round or based on the score from the previous hole.

Hook: A hook is a type of shot that curves the ball from right to left in the air, primarily affecting right-handed golfers. This occurs when the clubface is closed relative to the swing path at impact, causing the ball to spin in a way that results in this leftward trajectory. While a hook can generate additional distance due to topspin, it can also lead to undesirable outcomes, such as a severe misdirection known as a duck-hook. A less pronounced version of a hook is referred to as a draw or push-draw, which still curves left but with less severity.

Hosel: The hosel is an integral part of a golf club, specifically located at the top of the club head where the shaft is inserted. It serves as a connection point between the shaft and club head and can be described as an open hole or socket-like structure. In some designs, particularly those where the hosel and clubhead are manufactured as one piece, it may refer more broadly to this area.

Hosel Rocket: The term "hosel rocket" is slang for what is known as a shank in golfing terminology. A shank occurs when a player mishits the ball by striking it off the hosel of the club head rather than its face. This results in an erratic shot that travels very low and veers sharply to the right (for right-handed players), often leading to frustration for golfers.

Hybrid: A hybrid golf club combines features from both fairway woods and long irons, making it easier for players to hit than traditional long irons. Hybrids are designed with characteristics that enhance forgiveness and playability, allowing golfers to achieve better distance and accuracy from various lies on the course.

Impact Position: This refers to the alignment and posture of your body at the precise moment when your club strikes the ball. For optimal ball striking, various parts of your body—such as your hands, wrists, elbows, arms, shoulders, hips, and both upper and lower body—should be positioned according to established guidelines at the moment of impact.

In Play: After a golfer takes a shot from the tee box, the ball is considered "in play." It remains in this status until it is either successfully holed out, lost, marked, and lifted (when on the putting green), or struck out of bounds.

Interlocking Grip: This term describes a specific technique for gripping the golf club. In this method, the golfer interlaces their hands by placing the index finger of their lead hand between the pinky and ring fingers of their trailing hand. This creates an "interlocked" grip that can enhance control and stability during swings.

In the Leather: This term refers to a situation in golf where a short putt is considered so close to the hole that it can be conceded as made without actually being putted. Specifically, if the distance remaining for the putt is less than approximately 24 inches (the distance from the putter head to the bottom of the grip), it is said to be "in the leather." This concession is typically only applicable during friendly or unofficial rounds of golf.

Iron: The term "irons" encompasses all golf clubs with heads usually made of steel, designed for shots that are generally 200 yards or less, particularly for amateur players. Irons are distinct from woods, which are used primarily for longer shots such as drives.

Kick-In: A kick-in refers to an extremely short putt, often less than one foot from the hole, which is virtually impossible to miss. Due to its proximity, golfers typically consider these putts automatic.

Knee Knocker: This phrase describes a short putt that a golfer would normally expect to make but may feel anxious about due to pressure or nerves in critical moments. The psychological aspect of putting can turn what should be a straightforward shot into a challenging one.

Knickers: Often known as "Plus Fours," knickers are loose-fitting golf trousers that are cut short and gathered at the knee. These garments were particularly fashionable in the early 19th and 20th centuries but have largely fallen out of favor on modern golf courses.

Lag Putt: A lag putt refers to a long putt where the golfer does not realistically expect to make the shot. Instead, the objective is to get the ball as close to the hole as possible, minimizing the distance for the next putt.

Lateral Hazard: A lateral hazard is defined as a water hazard, such as a stream or pond, that runs alongside or parallel to the line of play towards the hole. These hazards are typically marked with red stakes on the golf course.

Launch Angle: The launch angle describes the angle at which a golf ball ascends vertically immediately after being struck by a club. This angle is measured in degrees relative to the ground and plays a crucial role in determining how high and far the ball will travel.

Lay Up: This is a strategic golf shot where the player intentionally strikes the ball a shorter distance than what might typically be expected. The purpose of this tactic is to steer clear of hazards or challenging areas on the course, thereby simplifying the next shot.

Lead Foot or Hand: This term describes the part of the golfer's body—be it foot, hand, or another area—that is closest to the target during the setup phase when preparing to hit the ball.

Level Par: This phrase indicates a score that matches the course's par. For instance, if a golfer completes a round with a score of 72 and the course par is also 72, that golfer is said to have achieved level par.

Line: In golf, this term refers to the theoretical trajectory on the putting green that extends from the golfer's ball to the hole, outlining how the putt will travel.

Lie: In golf, the term "lie" has two primary meanings. The first refers to the position of the golf ball in relation to the ground. For example, a ball that is sitting in thick grass or deep rough can be described as having a "thick lie," while a ball that is partially buried in the ground may be referred to as a "plugged lie." The second meaning pertains to the angle of the club shaft compared to the sole of the club, which affects how the club interacts with the ground during a swing.

Links: This term can denote flat European-style golf courses characterized by expansive greens. Additionally, it can simply refer to the act of playing a round of golf, regardless of course type.

Lip Out: A "lip out" occurs when a putt seems destined for success but veers off course at the last moment, failing to enter the hole. A less frustrating variant of this situation is known as a "burnt edge," where the ball grazes the edge of the hole but does not drop in.

Loft: The term "loft" describes the angle formed between the face of a golf club and the ground. Clubs with higher loft angles will launch the ball higher into the air upon impact, making loft an important factor in determining how far and high a shot will travel.

Long Game: The "long game" in golf refers to the category of shots that are executed from a distance greater than 100 yards from the green. This aspect of the game emphasizes power and accuracy, as players must navigate longer distances while considering factors such as wind, elevation changes, and course layout. In contrast, the "short game" encompasses all shots taken from within 100 yards of the green, focusing on precision and finesse.

Lost Ball: A lost ball is defined as one that a golfer cannot locate after it has been struck. According to the Rules of Golf, players are permitted to search for a lost ball for a maximum of three minutes. If the ball remains unfound after this period, specific procedures must be followed, including taking a penalty stroke and dropping a new ball in accordance with established rules.

LPGA: Teaching & Club Professional [T&CP] Division: This division represents a crucial segment of the Ladies Professional Golf Association (LPGA), which is recognized as one of the leading women's sports organizations globally. The T&CP Division focuses on promoting golf education and professional development for women in teaching and club management roles.

LPGA: Ladies Professional Golf Association: The LPGA is noted for being the longest-running women's sports association in history, having celebrated its 50th anniversary in 2000. It plays a vital role in advancing women's participation in golf at all levels, from amateur to professional competitions.

Match Play: Match play is a competitive format where individual players compete directly against one another rather than against an entire field. In this format, players earn points based on their performance on each hole; specifically, they receive one point for each hole won against their opponent.

Medal Play: Also known as "stroke play," medal play is a golf scoring format where the player totals all the strokes taken during their round. The final score is simply the cumulative number of strokes recorded.

Medalist: This term refers to the player who achieves the lowest gross score during qualifying rounds.

Mixed Foursome: This format involves teams that include both male and female golfers, typically consisting of two men and two women.

Mulligan: A mulligan allows golfers to retake a shot if they are dissatisfied with the initial outcome. While this practice is often accepted in casual games among friends, it is not permitted in official tournaments, where taking a mulligan would incur a penalty.

Nassau: This term refers to a specific type of wager in golf that combines three distinct bets into one. In a Nassau bet, participants place money on three outcomes: the best score on the front nine holes, the best score on the back nine holes, and the overall best score for the entire 18-hole round.

Net Score: A player's net score is calculated by totaling all strokes taken during a round or on individual holes and then subtracting the player's handicap from this total. The handicap is a numerical measure of a golfer's potential ability, allowing players of varying skill levels to compete fairly against one another.

Nineteenth Hole: This colloquial term refers to the bar or restaurant where golfers often gather after completing their round. It serves as a social hub for players to relax, discuss their game, and enjoy refreshments.

Open Face: In golfing terminology, an "open face" occurs when the club head is angled to the right of the target line at impact.

Additionally, it can describe a club head that is positioned significantly upward when preparing to execute a high lob shot.

Open Stance: An open stance describes a golfer's alignment at address where their feet and body are positioned so that they are aimed left of their intended target line. This stance can affect swing mechanics and shot trajectory.

Nassau: Out of Bounds

Golf courses typically feature markers such as ground stakes and fences that delineate the boundaries of the course. If a player's ball lands outside these designated indicators, it is considered "out of bounds."

Overlapping Grip: The overlapping grip is a technique for holding the golf club where the pinky finger of the lower hand rests in the groove between the index and middle fingers of the upper hand. This grip is sometimes known as the "Vardon grip," named after the famous golfer Harry Vardon.

Pace of Play: Pace of play refers to how quickly a group completes their round of golf. A common guideline is to maintain a speed that keeps you in line with the group ahead.

Pairing Sheet: A pairing sheet is a document that lists the pairings, or groups, of players participating in a tournament round of golf.

Pairings: Pairings refer to the individuals with whom players are grouped during a tournament round of golf.

Par: A golfer achieves a par on a hole when the number of strokes taken equals the par value assigned to that hole. For instance, if a golfer scores 4 on a hole designated as Par 4, this is considered a par score. Similarly, scoring 5 on a Par 5 hole also qualifies as a par.

Penalty Stroke: A penalty stroke is an additional stroke added to a player's score due to a violation of the rules. The specific situations that warrant these penalty strokes are outlined in the Rules of Golf, which detail various infractions and their corresponding penalties.

Pin: Commonly referred to as the "flag stick," the pin is a metal pole topped with a colored flag that marks the location of the hole on the green. This helps golfers gauge their distance from the hole during play.

Pin High: The term "pin high" describes an approach shot that lands at the same depth on the green as the flag stick. This indicates that the golfer has accurately judged the distance for their shot, landing it near where they intended.

Pitch Shot: A pitch shot is characterized as a short game shot typically played from approximately 40 to 60 yards away from the hole. It is executed with a high trajectory, allowing for minimal roll upon landing on the green due to its steep descent.

Pitch Mark: A pitch mark is an indentation created on the putting green when a golf ball lands. It is considered proper golf etiquette for players to repair any pitch marks they create to maintain the quality of the green.

PGA of America: Established in 1916, the PGA of America is the largest sports organization globally, with over 28,000 members dedicated to promoting golf across various demographics and regions.

PGA Tour: The PGA Tour refers to the professional golf tour that features many of the top golfers in the world, which is commonly broadcasted on television.

Pitch Shot: A pitch shot is a short golf shot characterized by a high trajectory that allows the ball to land softly on the green with minimal roll afterward.

Play Through: When golfers recognize that their pace of play is slower than expected and are holding up the group behind them, it is courteous for them to allow that group to "play through" by stepping aside and letting them proceed ahead.

Plugged Lie: This term describes a situation in golf where a ball becomes partially embedded in the ground after landing in its own pitch mark. According to the Rules of Golf, players are permitted to take relief without penalty from a plugged lie, with the exception of sand traps.

Plus Golfer: This term refers to an exceptionally skilled golfer whose handicap is less than zero. Unlike less skilled golfers who subtract their handicap strokes from their total score, a plus golfer must add strokes to their total score when participating in net events.

Practice Putting Green: This is a designated area on a golf course specifically set aside for players to practice their putting skills.

Preferred Lie: This term is used when course conditions are not optimal, prompting the manager or head professional to implement a local rule that allows players to improve their lie. This typically involves the "lift, clean, and place" rule, which permits players to lift their ball, clean it, and place it back in a more favorable position before making their shot.

Private Golf Course: A private golf course is one where access is limited strictly to members and their guests only, restricting play from the general public.

Provisional Ball: If you suspect that your ball may be lost or out of bounds after playing a shot, it is advisable to play a second ball immediately as a provisional. This approach is efficient because if you later find out that your original ball is indeed lost, you will not need to return to the original spot to hit again, thus saving time on the course.

Public Golf Course: A public golf course is one that allows members of the general public to play by paying a greens fee or daily fee. These courses are accessible to anyone who wishes to play golf, without the need for membership in a private club.

Push/Pull: Pushes and pulls refer to inaccurate golf shots that do not travel along the intended target line. For right-handed golfers, a push occurs when the ball travels to the right of the aimed target, while a pull occurs when it goes to the left. Typically, both types of shots result in straight ball flight rather than the curved trajectories associated with slices or hooks.

Punch Shot: A punch shot is characterized by a significantly lower trajectory than usual for a golf shot. This type of shot is often executed intentionally by players aiming to keep the ball beneath wind conditions or tree branches.

Putt: A putt is a specific type of golf shot executed when the ball is on the green. The player uses a specialized golf club known as a putter to strike the ball, aiming to make it roll smoothly along the ground toward the hole. The objective is to either sink the ball directly into the cup or position it very close to it for an easier subsequent shot.

Putter: The putter is the designated golf club utilized for making putts, particularly when the ball is on or in close proximity to the putting surface. This club is designed with a flat face and a heavier head compared to other clubs, allowing for precise control and accuracy needed for short-distance shots.

Quad Bogey: A quad bogey denotes a score that exceeds par by four strokes on any given hole. For instance, if a golfer scores 8 on a Par 4 hole, this would be classified as a quad bogey. Similarly, scoring 9 on a Par 5 hole would also result in a quad bogey.

Range: The term "range," abbreviated from "driving range," refers to an area designated for golfers to practice their swings. Driving ranges are typically located adjacent to golf courses and may be part of a larger golf club facility; however, they can also exist as independent commercial venues where golfers pay per bucket of balls to practice their skills.

Range Finder: A range finder is an electronic device designed to assist golfers in measuring the distance from their current position to a specific target on the golf course. These devices utilize laser technology, where a laser beam is directed towards the target. Upon reaching the target, the beam reflects back to the range finder, allowing it to calculate and display the precise yardage to that point. This technology enhances a golfer's ability to make informed decisions regarding club selection and shot strategy based on accurate distance measurements.

Reading The Green: Each putting green features various undulations and slopes, which can subtly influence the path of a golf ball as it rolls toward the hole. The process of analyzing these contours to predict how they will affect an upcoming putt is known as "reading the green." Golfers carefully observe factors such as slope direction, grain of the grass, and any imperfections on the surface that could alter the ball's trajectory. Mastering this skill is crucial for improving putting accuracy and overall performance on the green.

Ready Golf: To promote an efficient Pace of Play during rounds of golf, players within a group are encouraged to adopt a "ready golf" approach. This means that golfers should play their shots when they are prepared to do so, rather than adhering strictly to traditional order based on who is farthest from the hole. By allowing players to hit when ready, this practice can help reduce delays and keep the game moving smoothly.

Relief: In certain circumstances outlined by the Rules of Golf, players are permitted to move their ball without incurring a penalty. One common scenario is when a ball lies in an area designated as "ground under repair." When golfers reposition their ball according to these rules—such as moving it out of an unplayable lie or taking relief from obstructions—they are said to be "taking relief." Understanding when and how relief can be taken is essential for maintaining fair play and adhering to golfing regulations.

Re-load: This term is used in golf slang to describe the action of a player taking a second shot immediately after hitting a poor first shot. It is commonly referenced on the tee box, particularly when a golfer's initial tee shot goes out of bounds.

Resort: A golf course that is situated in a vacation or destination area, often associated with accommodations for visitors. These courses typically cater to tourists and may offer various amenities alongside golfing.

Reverse Pivot: In an ideal golf swing for right-handed players, weight is shifted to the right during the backswing and then transferred back to the left during the downswing. A "reverse pivot" occurs when this weight shift is performed incorrectly, meaning the player shifts their weight left on the backswing and right on the downswing.

Rough: This refers to areas of longer grass that border the fairways and extend from the tee box to the green. Golfers generally aim to avoid landing their ball in the rough due to its challenging playing conditions.

Round: The standard format of playing golf consists of eighteen holes.

Rub of the Green: The official definition of "rub of the green" refers to "the accidental deflection of a ball in motion by an outside agency." Over time, this term has evolved to encompass a broader interpretation, often used to signify any instance of bad luck experienced by a golfer during play.

Sand Trap: A sand trap is defined as a man-made depression filled with sand, strategically placed along fairways or near greens. These features are designed to increase the difficulty of play, compelling golfers to navigate around them. Players typically aim to avoid these hazards, which are also commonly known as "bunkers."

Sandbagger: This term is used derogatorily to describe a golfer who intentionally misrepresents their skill level by inflating their handicap. The purpose of this deception is to gain an unfair advantage in betting situations during competitive events.

Sand Save: This term describes the scenario where a golfer successfully makes par after hitting from a greenside bunker. Achieving this feat is often referred to colloquially as making a "sandy," highlighting the skill required to recover from such challenging positions on the course.

Sandy: A "sandy" refers to a situation in golf where a player successfully makes par after hitting their ball out of a greenside bunker. This achievement is often called a "sand save."

Scramble Format: In this format, each member of a team takes a tee shot. The team then selects the best shot among them and plays the next stroke from that location. This process continues, with the team repeatedly choosing the best shot until they hole out. The score for each hole is recorded, and the cumulative score is tallied as the team's overall score.

Seeding: Seeding involves arranging players in a draw based on their skill levels to ensure fair competition.

Scratch: A scratch golfer is an exceptionally skilled player whose handicap is 0, meaning they do not require any additional strokes to match the Course Rating on any golf course.

Skulled Shot: This term is synonymous with "bladed shot," which refers to a type of mishit where the ball is struck too high on the clubface, resulting in low trajectory and excessive distance.

Semi-Private Golf Course: A semi-private golf course has both members who pay for exclusive access and allows limited public play, providing a mix of private and public golfing experiences.

Shaft: The shaft of a golf club is the elongated, tapered tube that connects the grip to the club head. In general, shafts for drivers and fairway woods are predominantly constructed from graphite due to its lightweight and flexible properties, which can enhance swing speed and distance. Conversely, iron shafts are typically made from steel, providing greater durability and control.

Shank: The shank, often referred to as "The S Word" among golfers, is a particularly dreaded mishit. It occurs when the ball is struck off the neck or heel of the club, resulting in a shot that veers sharply to the right (for right-handed golfers). Shanks can be psychologically challenging for players because they are often perceived as contagious; many golfers believe that simply mentioning them can lead to an increased likelihood of experiencing one.

Short Game: The short game encompasses all types of shots executed within 100 yards of the green. This includes various techniques such as pitches (high shots with a soft landing), chips (low shots that roll out), bunker shots (played from sand traps), and putts (striking the ball on the green towards the hole). Mastery of the short game is crucial for lowering scores, as it involves precision and touch.

Short-Sided: The term "short-sided" describes a situation where a golfer hits an approach shot to the same side of the green where the pin is located. This positioning complicates subsequent chips or pitches because there is less green to work with for landing the ball softly before it rolls toward the hole.

Shot: In golf terminology, a shot refers to the action of striking a golf ball with a club. Each individual strike is considered either a shot or stroke, contributing to a player's overall score during a round.

Shotgun Start: A shotgun start is a golf tournament format where all groups of players begin their rounds simultaneously from different holes on the course. This method allows for a more efficient use of time, as it enables all participants to complete their rounds in a similar timeframe rather than waiting for each group to tee off sequentially from the first hole.

Skinny: The term "skinny" in golf refers to a mishit shot that occurs when the very bottom edge of the club face makes contact with the ball. This type of shot is also known as hitting the ball "thin." It typically happens when the golfer's club head moves upward through impact instead of descending at the correct angle. As a result, these shots often lead to lower trajectory and less distance than intended.

Skins: In a skins game, golfers compete within their foursome by aiming to achieve the lowest score on each hole. The player who has the lowest score on a hole wins that hole's "skin," which is usually associated with a predetermined monetary value (for example, $1 or $5). If multiple players tie for the lowest score on a hole, that skin carries over to the next hole, increasing its value.

Slice: A slice is a common problem faced by amateur golfers, characterized by a shot that curves dramatically from left to right in mid-air. This phenomenon occurs due to excessive sidespin imparted on the ball during impact, resulting in reduced distance and accuracy. A less severe version of this issue may be referred to as a cut or pull-cut.

Slope Rating: The slope rating quantifies the difficulty of a golf course specifically for amateur players, with values ranging from 55 to 155. A higher slope rating indicates a more challenging course.

Snowman: The term "snowman" is used in golf to describe a score of 8 on a player's scorecard. This term is derived from the visual appearance of the number 8, which resembles a snowman. Scoring a snowman can significantly affect a player's overall performance in a round.

Sole: The sole refers to the bottom part of a golf club's head that makes contact with the ground when the club is at address. It runs from the toe (the front part) to the heel (the back part) and includes both the leading edge (the front edge) and trailing edge (the back edge).

Slope: Slope is a numerical value that indicates how difficult a golf course is for a bogey golfer compared to a scratch golfer. This rating plays an essential role in calculating a golfer's handicap index, helping to level the playing field among golfers of varying skill levels.

Stableford: This is a scoring system used in golf where points are awarded based on the number of strokes taken on each hole, rather than simply counting total strokes. For example, a bogey (one stroke over par) earns 1 point, while a par (equal to par) earns 2 points, and a birdie (one stroke under par) earns 3 points. This system encourages players to play aggressively and can lead to more enjoyable rounds since it allows for better scoring opportunities even if a player has a bad hole.

Stance: The stance in golf refers to how a golfer positions their feet relative to each other when addressing the ball. It is typically categorized as square (feet parallel to the target line), open (front foot further from the target), or closed (back foot further from the target). Additionally, the stance can be described by how wide or narrow it is, which can affect balance and swing mechanics.

Sticks: In golfing slang, "sticks" refers to golf clubs. This informal term is commonly used among golfers when discussing their equipment or during casual conversations about the game.

Stimpmeter: The stimpmeter is an instrument designed to measure the speed of putting greens. It resembles a yardstick with a V-shaped groove along its length. To use it, one end of the stimpmeter is elevated while a golf ball is rolled down its track onto the green. The distance that the ball travels on the putting surface determines the Stimp Rating for that green, providing valuable information about its speed for players and course managers alike.

Stinger: A stinger is a specific type of golf shot characterized by a very low trajectory. This shot is typically executed from the tee box and is particularly useful in situations where there is a headwind or when the ground conditions are firm, allowing the ball to roll significantly after landing.

Stroke: In golf, the term "stroke" refers to the action of striking the golf ball with a club. It can also be referred to as a shot.

Stroke Play: Stroke play is a format of golf where the total score for a completed stipulated round is counted. This format is commonly known as "medal play."

Strong Grip: A strong grip in golf involves positioning the hands on the club such that the 'V' shapes formed between the thumbs and forefingers point towards the golfer's right shoulder. Additionally, this grip allows the golfer to see more than two knuckles of their left hand at address.

Superintendent: The superintendent is responsible for maintaining the golf course, ensuring its overall health and playability. This individual may also be referred to as the greenskeeper.

Sweet Spot: The sweet spot refers to a specific area on the club face of a golf club that optimally transfers energy to the golf ball upon impact. When the ball strikes this precise location, it results in minimal vibration felt in the club, leading to a more effective and powerful shot.

Swing: In golf, the full swing encompasses a series of intricate and coordinated movements executed by the golfer to strike the ball. This sequence includes four main components: the backswing (the initial movement away from the ball), the downswing (the motion bringing the club down towards the ball), the follow-through (the continuation of movement after hitting the ball), and finally, the finish (the position at which the swing concludes).

Swing Path: This term describes the trajectory or direction in which the club head travels as it approaches and makes contact with the golf ball. Swing paths can be categorized into three primary types: "outside-in" (where the club moves from outside to inside relative to the target line), "inside-out" (where it moves from inside to outside), and "down the line" (where it travels straight along the intended target line).

Swing Plane: The swing plane is an imaginary flat surface that represents the angle formed during both backswing and follow-through. It serves as a guide for maintaining proper swing mechanics, helping golfers achieve consistency in their shots.

Takeaway: The takeaway is the initial phase of the backswing in golf, beginning when the club head is positioned behind the ball at address. This phase continues until the club reaches a point where it is parallel to the ground and aligned with the target path, a position referred to as double parallel.

Tap In: A tap-in is a very short putt that is considered nearly impossible to miss. It is often colloquially known as a gimme or a kick-in, indicating that it requires minimal effort to complete.

Tee: A tee is a small device made of wood or plastic that elevates the golf ball off the ground. Tees are primarily used when playing from the tee box at the start of each hole.

Tee Box [or teeing ground]: The tee box is a specific area on each golf course hole designated for players to take their first shot. Most courses feature multiple tee boxes per hole, allowing golfers of varying skill levels to select the most suitable option for their game.

Tee Shot: A tee shot refers to the first stroke taken from the tee box on every hole, marking the beginning of play for that particular hole.

Tee Time: This refers to the scheduled time for starting a round of golf. For instance, if you have a tee time at nine o'clock, it indicates that you should be ready to tee off on the first hole at exactly 9:00 AM.

Tempo: This term describes the rhythm and pace of a golfer's swing, which can be somewhat subjective. It is often characterized by descriptors such as fast, slow, or smooth. Each golfer has a unique tempo that reflects their individual style and approach to swinging the club.

Tending The Flag: Historically in golf, it was required to remove the flagstick from the hole before a putt could be made. This process involved a playing partner holding the flagstick while another player putted and then removing it as the ball approached the hole. This action was known as "tending the flag."

Texas Wedge: This is a colloquial term used when a golfer chooses to use their putter for a shot taken from off the green instead of using a wedge for chipping. It typically occurs when the ball is close enough to the green that putting is deemed more effective than chipping.

Thin: The optimal golf shot occurs when the club face makes contact with the bottom part of the ball, which is resting on the ground. However, due to various swing imperfections, golfers may strike the ball higher up, near its equator. This type of mishit is commonly referred to as hitting the ball "thin."

The Tips: Golf courses typically feature multiple tee boxes. The forward tees are designed to provide an easier and shorter route to the hole, while the back tees, known as "the tips," present a more challenging and longer path. It is generally recommended that only the most skilled players attempt to play from these back tees.

The Turn: An 18-hole golf course is divided into two sections: the front nine (the first nine holes) and the back nine (the last nine holes). When a player finishes playing the front nine and prepares to start on the back nine, this transition is referred to as "making the turn."

Tight Lie: A "tight lie" occurs when a golfer's ball rests in an area with minimal grass beneath it. This sparse turf can complicate shots for amateur players, who often prefer having some grass cushioning under their ball for better contact.

Toe: The toe of a golf club refers to the area of the club face that is located beyond the grooves and is farthest from the golfer when addressing the ball. This part of the club is critical for understanding how different impacts can affect ball flight. In contrast, the opposite end of the club face is known as the "heel," which is closer to the golfer.

Topped Shot: A topped shot occurs when a golfer strikes the top half of the ball with the bottom edge of the club. This mis-hit results in a shot that typically travels only a short distance, often just a few yards, and can be quite frustrating for players as it fails to achieve intended distance or accuracy.

Trail Foot or Hand: The term "trail foot" or "trail hand" refers to the part of a golfer's body that is farthest from the target during their setup position when preparing to hit the ball. For right-handed golfers, this would be their right foot and right hand, while for left-handed golfers, it would be their left foot and left hand. Understanding this positioning is essential for proper swing mechanics.

Triple Bogey: A triple bogey, commonly referred to as a "trip," occurs when a golfer completes a hole with a score that is three strokes over par. For example, if a hole has a par of 4, scoring 7 on that hole would result in a triple bogey. This term reflects performance relative to par and can impact overall scoring in a round.

Unplayable Lie: An unplayable lie refers to a situation where a golfer's ball is in play but positioned in such a way that making an effective swing or advancing it becomes impossible. In such cases, golfers have the option to declare their ball unplayable according to the Rules of Golf. Once declared unplayable, there are three relief options available, all requiring taking one penalty stroke before proceeding with play.

Up: In match play, a player who has won more holes than they have lost is considered to be "up" in the match. For instance, if a player has won five holes and lost four, that player is "one up."

Up and Down: This term refers to a situation where a player does not reach the green in regulation (which is two strokes under par for that hole) but successfully pitches the ball onto the green and then holes it in one additional stroke.

Uphill Lie: An uphill lie occurs when a player's ball rests on an uneven surface, specifically when their front foot is positioned higher than their back foot due to the slope of the ground.

USGA: The acronym stands for the United States Golf Association, which serves as the governing body for golf in both the United States and Mexico. The USGA oversees the national handicap system and is responsible for producing and interpreting the Rules of Golf.

USGTF: The acronym stands for the United States Golf Teachers Federation, which is recognized as the largest organization globally dedicated to the intensive training and certification of elite golfers. Its primary mission is to prepare individuals to teach and coach golfers across all levels of skill, age, gender, and ethnicity. Upon successful completion of its courses, the USGTF awards a diploma of certification. To maintain this certification, members must remain in good standing within the organization.

Vardon Grip: This grip style is named after Harry Vardon, a renowned British golfer active during the late 19th and early 20th centuries. Vardon was instrumental in popularizing this particular grip technique, which is commonly known today as the "overlapping" grip. This method involves overlapping the little finger of the trailing hand over the index finger of the leading hand, providing stability and control during a golf swing.

Waggle: A waggle refers to a small movement that golfers perform to help alleviate tension before addressing the ball. Typically, this motion consists of one to three gentle waggles that serve as a way for players to relax and focus before executing their shot.

Winter Rules: This term describes a local rule that allows players to improve their lie within designated areas due to adverse course conditions typically associated with winter weather. Under winter rules, golfers may be permitted to clean or move their ball in order to ensure fair play despite challenging conditions on the course.

Watery Grave: This term refers to a situation in golf where a player hits their ball into a body of water, such as a pond or lake. The phrase likens the water to a grave, suggesting that the ball has found its final resting place there.

Weak Grip: A weak grip in golf is characterized by the positioning of the hands on the club such that the 'V' shapes formed between the thumbs and forefingers point towards the left shoulder (for right-handed golfers). This grip can lead to undesirable outcomes, particularly for amateur players, often resulting in a slice—a shot that curve dramatically to the right.

Whiff: In golfing terminology, a "whiff" occurs when a golfer attempts to strike the ball but completely misses it. This can happen due to poor timing or misjudgment during the swing.

Wood: The term "wood" refers to any golf club that traditionally had a wooden head. In modern times, however, these clubs are typically constructed from metal composites. Woods are designed for long-distance shots and are generally used for teeing off or hitting from fairways.

Worm Burner: A "worm burner" is slang for a poorly executed shot where the ball either barely lifts off the ground or remains entirely on the ground after being struck. This type of shot is often unintentional and indicates an error in technique.

X-outs: These are golf balls that are typically sold at a reduced price due to minor cosmetic imperfections that occur during the manufacturing process.

Yank: This term describes a golf shot that veers offline to the left, commonly referred to as a "pull."

Yardage: This term indicates the distance between the golfer's ball and their intended target.

Yips: The yips are a frustrating condition in golf characterized by involuntary muscle spasms or mental blocks that disrupt a golfer's ability to execute fundamental tasks. This issue primarily affects putting, leading to erratic swing motions that can negatively impact the shot.

Zip: This term refers to the backspin applied to the golf ball upon impact, which causes it to stop quickly when it lands on the green or, in some cases, even roll backward.

More recommended reading:

Ultimate Guide to Golf, The Journey Begins
Optimizing The Golf Swing—Biomechanics
Golfopedia Front Nine, Back Nine & 19th Tee - Trilogy
Golden Greens, Golfing Through Life's Back Nine
Golf Made Easy – Before Your First Round
Mind Over Mulligans, Mastering Your Mindset
Scoring Magic, Transform Your Short Game Today

Epilogue:
Wrapping Up

As we conclude this guide, it's worth reflecting on the remarkable journey that lies ahead for both parents and junior golfers. The path of junior golf is more than just a series of rounds played, or tournaments entered—it's an extraordinary opportunity for growth, connection, and character development that extends far beyond the fairways and greens.

Throughout this guide, we've explored the multifaceted aspects of supporting a young golfer, from understanding the technical elements of the game to nurturing the mental fortitude required for success. Yet perhaps the most valuable lesson is that the true measure of success in junior golf isn't found solely in scorecards or tournament victories, but in the life skills and values developed along the way.

For parents embarking on this journey with their children, remember that your role is pivotal but should be balanced. The most successful junior golf experiences often come when parents learn to be supportive without being overbearing, encouraging without adding pressure, and present without being intrusive. Your guidance helps shape not just a golfer, but a person who understands dedication, resilience, and sportsmanship.

Looking ahead, the landscape of junior golf continues to evolve, offering more opportunities than ever before. Whether your child dreams of collegiate golf, professional competition, or simply enjoys the game for its lifelong recreational value, the foundation built during these formative years will serve them well in whatever path they choose.

As you close this book and step onto the course with your junior golfer, carry with you the understanding that every round, every practice session, and every moment shared is contributing to something far greater than the game itself. Golf, with its unique blend of individual challenge and character-building opportunities, provides an unparalleled platform for young people to develop into confident, capable individuals.

May your journey in junior golf be filled with moments of joy, growth, and shared success, always remembering that the greatest victory isn't found in perfect shots or winning scores, but in the remarkable person your young golfer becomes along the way.

About the Author:

Certified Golf Professional and Inventor

Glen Bowen is a Certified Professional Golf Coach, affiliated with the United States Golf Teachers Federation (USGTF) and the United States Golf Association (USGA). With over two decades of experience, he provides personalized golf instruction in Salado, (Central) Texas.

Bowen is inventor of the Firecracker® golf tee, which was awarded "Best in Class" by Golf Test USA in competition with other leading tees and is approved by the USGA for tournament play.

He served as a medic in the U.S. Air Force during the Vietnam War and later was bestowed with an honorary commission as Admiral in the Texas Navy by Governor Rick Perry for his contributions to Texas.